NUER-ENGLISH DICTIONARY

NUER-ENGLISH DICTIONARY

Huffman, Ray

www.General-Books.net

Publication Data:

Title: Nuer-English Dictionary
Author: Huffman, Ray
Reprinted: 2010, General Books, Memphis, Tennessee, USA
Publisher: Berlin D. Reimer
Publication date: 1929
Subjects: Nuer language – Dictionaries English

How We Made This Book for You
We made this book exclusively for you using patented Print on Demand technology.
First we scanned the original rare book using a robot which automatically flipped and photographed each page.
We automated the typing, proof reading and design of this book using Optical Character Recognition (OCR) software on the scanned copy. That let us keep your cost as low as possible.
If a book is very old, worn and the type is faded, this can result in numerous typos or missing text. This is also why our books don't have illustrations; the OCR software can't distinguish between an illustration and a smudge.
We understand how annoying typos, missing text or illustrations, foot notes in the text or an index that doesn't work, can be. That's why we provide a free digital copy of most books exactly as they were originally published. You can also use this PDF edition to read the book on the go. Simply go to our website (www.general-books.net) to check availability. And we provide a free trial membership in our book club so you can get free copies of other editions or related books.
OCR is not a perfect solution but we feel it's more important to make books available for a low price than not at all. So we warn readers on our website and in the descriptions we provide to book sellers that our books don't have illustrations and may have numerous typos or missing text. We also provide excerpts from each book to book sellers and on our website so you can preview the quality of the book before buying it.
If you would prefer that we manually type, proof read and design your book so that it's perfect, simply contact us for the cost. We would be happy to do as much work as you would be like to pay for.

Limit of Liability/Disclaimer of Warranty:
The publisher and author make no representations or warranties with respect to the accuracy or completeness of the book. The advice and strategies in the book may not be suitable for your situation. You should consult with a professional where appropriate. The publisher is not liable for any damages resulting from the book.
Please keep in mind that the book was written long ago; the information is not current. Furthermore, there may be typos, missing text or illustration and explained above.

NUER-ENGLISH DICTIONARY

Foreword.

The words tabulated here have been collected from every source to which I have had access during the four and one-half years I have spent in Nuerland.

Words have been given me by other missionaries, those contained in the school books as well as those which I have learned directly from the Nuers themselves during my residence among them, have been listed.

After the first draft of this dictionary was made, every word was reviewed with the help of from one to six Nuers and this book as published is the final result.

All words marked with an asterisk are spelled as given me by Prof. D. Westermann of the International Institute of African Languages and Cultures who worked with one Nuer man at the Rejaf Language Conference at Rejaf, Sudan in 1928.

The singular form of nouns is first given, followed by the plural form (if known).

All open vowels have been marked in this dictionary because it is for the use of the European but I do not urge the marking of the open A, I, and u in books for the Nuer as the eight vowels a, e, i, o, u, e, o and o are sufficient.

The Nuer tribe is large and various estimates are made as to their number. At the Rejaf Language Conference in 1928, their number was given as 430,000.

They occupy a large area in the southern part of the Anglo-Egyptian Sudan, along the Sobat liver in the Nasser and Abwong districts and on the Zeraf island and along the Nile river.

Little has been published about this pagan tribe by those who have lived among them for any time. But little has been done to reduce the language of this illiterate tribe to writing. There are several dialects but the differences are slight. This language is rich in folklore. The words given here are but a small portion of what one may hope to find.

I am deeply indebted to my Nuer teachers, especially to Dhiel Rwac and Pec Kak for their patience, to Reverend W. J. Adair of the American Mission at Nasser for his constant encouragement, and to Prof. D. Westermann of the International Institute of African Languages and Cultures for his valuable advice and assistance in preparing this book for the publisher.

Rav Huffman

American Mission Nasser, Sudan-

Nuer alphabet as adopted at the Rejaf Language Conference April 1928 and used in this book. b as in English. d as in English.

g as in English "go" and "got". k as in English. I as in English. m as in English. n as in English. p as in English. r trilled lingual r. t as in English. w as in English "water". y consonantal as in English "yet". c palatalized t, almost as ch in "church". j palatalized d, approaching j in "judge", resembling dy. dh interdental d. th interdental t. nh interdental n.

ny palatalized n as gn in French "Boulogne". I) velar n. Y velar fricative voiced resembling Arabic ghain.

VOWELS.

a as in Italian; e, i, 0, u are close vowels.

e open e as in French "pere", or in English "let".

0 open o as in English "not" as distinct from "note".

0 central vowel resembling e in English "father".

Long or doubled vowels are represented by doubling the letter.

When a word changes when a suffix has been added, the original spelling has been retained in most cases. When needing a very slight u, have used w. When needing a very slight i, have used y. Besides the sounds described, above the language has an open i and u as in

"fit" and "put", they are represented by I and u, and the sound of u in "but", this is rendered bv A.

Nuer-English Dictionary.

a when.

a, kwa let (sing.) a ku te you let it alone; (pi.) kwa te you let it alone. a participle, sign of passive voice, infinitive. abe, abeeni lie is coming. Adam Adam, ay an exclamation. ajor absent.

alla exclamation of surprise. alenu what is it? a math slow, slowly. arath for a long distance. athin there is. au world.

mi au ci kaq kwony full moon. au cuol evening about 7 p. m. au mai fishing season. awano here. awui cry of distress or sorrow, used by men only.

baan bedbugs.

bac slovenly.

badak eight.

badakdien eighth.

bailoc one class of Nuers, now old men about 60 years old. bak to call to go together.

bak early morning before sunrise; dawn. bakcl six. bakellicn sixth.

bal (cike jc bal) to go on ahead of. bal to overleap. bal to pass by. bam vulva.

ban to run; fast; speed, bany prosperous; rich. bany piny to leave on ground; to abandon. bai) excuse (cue bar) CO cap) he plotted excuse; empty; free; false; for nothing. bai), barjni veranda; porch, barjbel one kind of white dura. baqwan nine. baqwandicn ninth. bap breast, including chest and stomach. bap to fall forward; to run aimlessly. bapdit sea.

bap milual redbreast. bap rar to break down. bar, ban good dancer. bar, bareni long, longer. bar Anuak (ran bar, jl bar); large pool; lake. bar to shoot; to run away; to fly;.

to flee; to send for; to send a thing; bow and arrow. bara bamia. ban stature.

baro baro seven; constellation of seven stars. barodien seventh. bat to mark; to check with pencil; to cross out with pencil; to swallow. jl bat A fishhook and line. bath famine. bath to be lost. ram mi bath bath deserter. bau war evening or morning star. ba also.

ba shall; I shall. babur steamer; boat. bak to cut open; to split open. b A ken Ike seeing them or visiting them for awhile. bak ke to divide in parts. bak- wic headache. bal, b All donkey; mule. balle tasteless. balle thu very tasteless. be dowry, when they bring all the cattle to bride's place. bee uncomfortable feeling; to hurt; hurt; pain. bee to spy out; to long for; to yearn after. bee wanted to kill ox in village in order to keep meat for self. berj kernel in groin or axilla. ber line; rafters; window casing, cross pieces. be would; shall (3d. pers. sing.); also 3d. person singular of bir. bel, poss.

beel dura; kaffir corn. bel to make peace beleni ro (they make peace themselves); to lick; (ku ro bel, jin karo) used to mean it is your own fault.

bel n. arbitration.

bl ben ke bende to come on one's own accord. bet to shake as ca tetda bet (I shook my hand). Beth lee m Bethlehem. bi, bieni clothes; garment. bi mi te maan best clothes. bi mi yath yath sackcloth; mourning garments. bi mi yual woolen goods. bie big mound in Lau part of

Nuerland made by? underj, blown up by government in 1927 28. bier markings on body for beauty; v. to mark body for beauty. bier- (biereni je) to bind house with grass. biel, biel color; biel mi mer purple; mi yen yellow; mi lit brownish black; mi lual red. biel duop mouse. biet to keep silence; bin I 2nd. pers.

sing, imperative; biete 2nd.

pers. pi. imperative. biet cataract. biet blessing.

bil cut (used for smaller cuts). bil blacksmith; potter: fault. bil to taste: to open, used as CI nhial bil meaning the clouds scattered leaving the sky clear, bim to eavesdrop. bio club with head. bi, bike will.

biam to waylay; to lie in wait. bldit, bldit quack of wild ducks. blka will become; cika became. bir 2nd. pers. sing, imperative.

bure bea come, 2nd. pers. pi. imperative.

bia come, 2nd. pers. pi. imperative.

ben came. bir cor come closer imperative (sing.) bit- to curse. blth fishing spear. boam to hug. bol was heated and smells; coals of fire; white-haired. boll sunbeams; sun near sunset. bon long dance dress. bon, bunni pelican. bon partition. bony to go under water; to dive; one kind of red dura. bor lap of person; white; to hover over. both to lead. both daddy-long-legs. bou fruit of sunt tree, Nuers pound fruit and make pancakes. bo ye white; bright. bo ye pak very white. bor kwe thorns put on calf's mouth to keep it from sucking. bot- to menstruate. bot, boni sore, wound, abscess; jl buoni the ones who have sores. both to lead with a rope. both tocka to drag. both hunger. both e nak hungry; both ke nak both nei nak; they are hungry, we are hungry; both ye nak you are hungry. bua chapped; cold sores caused by wind. buai light.

buau, poss. buoka sunt tree; bue, bui bell made from doleib nut.

bum able-bodied; courageous; hard; power. bum etet, bumketet very hard; very strong. buok rotten (used with things in house). buol to rot. buom strength.

buoka cai) middle of afternoon. buon, buonni group; herd; crowd; company. buor grass at bank of river; buor- to make fun of. buor windbreak for fire. buot tree, possibly shrub; cotton armlet; certain ornament. buoth to crawl; to creep. buoth, buorjl goat. buoye, buoyeni fishnet. bup to turn upside down. but to stay all day. but ke luai to file in slowly. but but bush with thorns. buth small melon; manure pile. buk to assemble; to throw at; to besmear; to thrust; to spread over surface. buk ethur to make commotion. bul to heat or roast over hot open fire; to toast; to roast; festival; toast; trunk of body. bul bul- wasp nest (Nuers moisten it with water and feed to cow for certain illness). bul, poss. bwol dance, drum. bul thuor dance but not wedding dance. bure, bure to call pussy, pussy.

buth buth to deceive; to plaster; smash as of falling body hitting floor, (used with big things only).

buth sterile (female only).

bwony to dive.

bwok weeds.

bwum when part of generative organs are undeveloped.

cac abreast in a row.

Cagi Abbysinians, part of whom raided Nuerland. cai exclamation of surprise. cai yatni class of Nuers, tribal marks made in 1925, also called wum kcluqka. cak- to put; milk. cam north; left hand. cam- to eat; to cheat. cam cam iodine. can destitute; forlorn; sad; poor. can can entirely full. cai) sun; even if. caijdar noon. caije right now.

CI cai) nei luot sunshine warmed us. ci cai) rode bak about 1 p. m. pai cai) thai warm a little in sunshine. cai) kany sunrise; east. caqke to refuse them when there is nothing good. cai) kwony sunset; west. cany bad food; to abhor; bad; finicky about eating; to sort out the best. canyc jc to refuse to have anything to do with person on account of sores; prissy.

gwan canya abhorrer.

cap plot; fault.

cap cap to plan: to plot.

car to view: considerate; to consider; to look around; to ponder; road; thought; worry; consideration.

car kler big aquatic animal, fine skin.

mi car, ticar black.

carboc one class of Nuers now about 30 35 years old.

carl twok wic table set the table.

cau to make splashing sound; cikc WA cau they went splash or as we say made a splashing sound.

CAk creator; formation; creation; tick.

CAk to fabricate; to create; to make; to start a fire.

CAk kwoth freak.

CAk- cuk to parade; to drill.

CAl, cai groin.

CAl, CAt resembles, is like.

cai), mn day.

cai) cdan, (pi.) nm ti kon one day awhile back; from 5 8 days ago.

CAl) kel sometime in future.

cai) jec lat Monday; cai) lat da-reudlen Tuesday; caij lat dyokdien Wednesday; CAl) lat nwandien Thursday; CAl) lat dhyecdicn Friday; caij lat mitot Saturday; CAl) kwoth Sunday.

mi car car level as rol mi car CAr (level country).

CAt, to slip; (3d. per. sing, past) ce cot.

CAt CAt slippery.

cuai) cck ripe eel, poss. cecl big fish.

cei) to live at; to abide.

ccij- bi pwony to dress.

cerja life; cei)Ada my life.

ceij-ro a gwaa to visit nicely; friendly.

ciel to peel cane or cornstalks.

ciem- to kiss.

cicm kiss.

ciemani his family; ciemori your family; ciemandlen their family; ciemari my family; cie-manniklen their families.

cien pity; compassion.

ciene very small fish, (like than).

cier pietha southern cross.

cier comet; planet; animal resembling cat that always bites at everything it touches.

cieth dung; feces.

cili), ciiqni village; town.

jl cili) villagers; inhabitants.

ciin-thu family-in-law.

cim- to whip.

CI sign of negative; sign of past, perfect tense.

cic, ceni the same as.

cieke, pi. cuie smaller, shorter.

Clep long grass skirt.

clka became; bik a become.

Clkc; cuo they.

Cll, del elbow.

cin, cin bowels; intestines.

Cll) bad as when fish is rotten; used for very bad as spoiled fish smells badly.

Cin mi cuo cuo small intestine; cin mi dhok dhok large intestine.

cir cir, cir cirni centipede.

Clt, Clteke, cite, CAt equally; like; the same as. Clthe diarrhea; to have diarrhea. CO and, connecting sentences. CO husband; (her) coade; urine; WA com lac to urinate. coi very nice: very good. col- to return borrowed money. conyict fiance; bridegroom. cop dura planter (stick with one end like spoon for making holes for planting dura); to reach, ci pi cop piny water covered ground. cor, cur, adj. cor blind. COrial black and white ox without horns; animal like waterbuck. cok image: stingy; small black worm that eats dura. cok person. col- to call. col open part of ear; part of snail shell. cot, cot, poss. cotnl boys who have just had the tribal marks cut. COt hornless. cot cotnl cow without horns, will turn into Let. cot-ro to line up single file. cotdul one kind of red dura. cot rial, cot riall zebra, cu, cwaye negative, do not. cuac to drive.

cuak, cuak, poss. cuakni twins. cual, cuah sack. cual poor dancer. cuane do not (includes person speaking) l 8t pers. pi. cuany ox.

cuai) to be perplexed be wiede cuai); to kill time te cuai) cuai)- cuai e cuar) cwa leet cuai) e cuai) continually changing his order. cuatcuor certain class of Nuers of long ago, all dead now. cuath fat; to start a fire; to make a bonfire. cue tired. cue, ce he; she; it. cue, cui leech. cuel penis; to squat. cuer one kind of white dura, cuer, ram mi cuer, nei ti cuer thief. cueth place where guinea worm comes out of; moonbeams; sunbeams; reached the ground. CUle narrow, cull to be very tired of; to be worn out entirely. cult to hiss; to insert. cuk part of; earthern cooking pot. cuk, cukni foot, cul clear water in river or well so you can see bottom. cul a god, sender of dreams, cul cuek calf of leg; muscles of arm or lower part of leg. cum cum sweet, delicious. cume dear; delicious; tastes good, used with other things than food. cui) to stop; to draw up; correct. cut)A height. cui) cui) good; straight. cui)-dor to hide. cui epic straight; perfect; absolutely good. cui) (jok) to sit up; (cuk) to stand on heel. curjka standing. cui)ni, curje you keep quiet.

cui) tet ligament.

pwanykien cuo cuo very muscular.

cuok to press upon; to crowd; to sit close, touching; to bump into each other.

cuo I revenge; recompense; dirt; to repay.

cuol, cul e cue darkness; very dark.

wai)- cuol to be blinded, as when going into dark room out of bright light.

cuom to encourage; savour.

cuom angry now, afterwhile will be very angry; quarrel.

cuo cuoni bronchial tubes; capillaries.

cuop (cuk) ankle area; (tet) wrist.

cuoth- to rub; to polish.

cuoko we.

cuorj; goie righteousness.

cuor vulture.

cuor mi rial very large buzzard.

cuor when hair is partly grey.

cuot large intestine; to put in an enclosed place.

cup to reach; to arrive at.

cur n. blind.

cut, cuut name.

cut to drag; to fall; to call; recompense.

cut ryai smokestack of boat.

cut piny to be lost.

cuth eraser.

cuut- pacifier for child.

cum snail; snailshell.

cumcie fine copper wire.

cwa bone.

cwa buom sacrum and coccyx.

cwa jok vertebral column.

cwa leet dorsal vertebrae.

cwaye deman cwaye tender as meat is tender.

ewe one kind of worm.

cwec south; right hand.

cwei gravy; soup.

cweny liver.

cwel to circumcise.

cwol name of man.

cwoth guinea worm: disease carried by guinea worm. CWOC weariness.

CWOIJ to abate; smoothly; straight. cyai) habit; mid it patience. cyat cyai) daily. cyek man, poss. cyik, mam wife. cyek fertile; chain; anklet; bracelet; wristlet; finger ring. cyek cyek short, small of stature. cyek jok widow. cyek mi kau young woman as yet childless. cyo(k)de his foot.

dai dai warm: lukewarm, as pi tl dai dai warm water. dai vacant; no one there; A Ia dai desolate. dak cannot reach; to pillage; to tear down; to plunder; to destroy; to abolish; to put out; to separate. dak ro to get a divorce. dak n. divorce; heartburn. dak piny to scatter; to disperse. dai to rub. dai) wedding stick. dai)e puffer fish that is slippery, has false and true skin.

daqkeni to sorape all flesh off of hide so it will dry well. dai) ro some come: some go. dap n. birth; to give birth (used for humans only); to bear children. dap jor to abort. dapni right now. dar amidst; middle; zenith. dar, poss. dwar idiot. dar dwar or dar doar middle of field; desert; uncultivated area; uninhabited place; wilderness. dare top of head. dareudlen second. dany- to hold out hands in amazement.-da suffix meaning my.-dan suffix meaning ours. daf) to remove bad part; to operate. darjdl how much; to the number of. mi dar red.

dar one kind of red dura. da(r)dar greedy; stingy. ram mi da(r)dar elorj sponger. dat sore between cow's toes. de able; can; should; would; shall; might; could; fruit. de jiath fruit of tree. dec n. wrinkles. dec- to choke; to strangle. dec- to overcome you because too heavy. der to hold burden on head without handling it.-de suffix meaning its, hers, his. del, det, poss. deel, deet sheep. del kwoth butterfly. things).

del del thick, big, large (used with deman, demani brother; demar, deman my brother; demor, dcqcek demon your brother; dcmandicn their brother. dcqcck bad snake, green and white. dcp- to annoy; to fish; to accuse; to implicate; to tease. dcp n. rope.

gwan dcp, poss. deep fisherman. dep wan shoestrings. deth- to carry. diar gourd with neck. diem the country that lies beyond; different. dieq to fish (with spear and string). dier iron beams used to support bridge. die maybe, diel antelope.

diem to strain as strain milk. dier wild animal; to fill in low places with dirt. dier, dicn pig. dieth to beget; to calve; to give birth to (used with animals). dicthke parents; ancestors. run tl diethke Jithath life of Jesus. run tl kon tl dicthke jc life. dil to stop up crevices; to fill up; to mend; numb. dil dil cannot see. dioq to mix; grass which is cooked. din inlet in river (not natural). dit, diit song. dit, di(t)ni roofer. dit, comp. ditni big; large; great. dit grown up; anxious; to esteem; greedy in every way dit loc; envious. dit, dif, poss. din bird. ram mi dit Iwac covetous person. diu doubt.

diu- to doubt.

dial all.

-dlcn suffix meaning theirs, (added to all numerals except 'six where-hen is used, to make adjective out of noun as making two 'second.

dlk certain grass, seed used for food.

dil perhaps; complete; persistently; master; favorite; aristocracy of Nuers, certain family and all related.

din now: surely: exactly.

dil) to sink.

dir to fertilize; to entice; to tempt; to make trial; to obstruct; nose stopped up; cold in head or lungs; return of feeling after numbness; deaf; always concerned about others; responsible.

do, de the young of anything; offspring; lamb do dcel; de deet; calf do yaij, deyok; core of sore.

doc to wither.

dor, poss. dar dwar (or) doar steppe: bush: open spaces; wilderness.

dol- tok to laugh.

dominyal calf with red spotted body.

dompiny night dance.

donpiny peanuts.

dony to crush; to nudge; to step on.

dony bul kingfisher.

do; dot) perhaps; maybe.

do bwol small drum.

dodicn, kokien other; another.

dok bead, large, white, oblong.

dolcni thulbuk collecting taxes.

doij- ro to roll about; to be restless.

dongorjka dwoth dongoqka class of Nuers about 40 years old now.

doq- to rap; to sift; to collect the good only out of anything.

dor) bracelet made of many little rings of ostrich shell.

doi), poss. duq n. knock; rap.

dop- to start fire.

du, dwaye do not.

du, ce wa du (it went calm) or (it is calm) no wind; calm.

-du,-dun suffix meaning yours.

dual to nod.

duany- to beckon by winking.

duany ni pon (may nothing harm you) special blessing.

duaq, mi duaq duaq aged; old.

dual) tet tendon in elbow.

duar to refuse what is offered; same as "brother" when speaking to younger person.

due to dodge.

dui try me out.

dul long hair; cornsilk; dirt; clod of dirt.

dulc bleached hair.

dull bricks to hold pot off fire.

dun to fall or ebb; dry.

duq of; very; if.

duq, nyin belonging to; belongings; possessions.

duol store; to assemble; n. congregation.

duop flesh in bridge of nose.

duor to hold tightly.

du(r)dur early morning; dawn.

dut, poss. dwot grass used for roofing, also called geu.

duth child which is weaned; to wean; free gift; to pull stick out of spear; to dance; to take up cattle stakes. dwac to beat; to whip. dwac gcr to eat. dwal to fear; to be afraid; fear. dwal sheepskin as garment, worn over woman's shoulder. dwalc lazy; dwal pwony to be indisposed. ram mi dwal dwal coward. dwany, dwanyi born a cripple. dwany- to bend; entirely good. dwaq breeze; air. ram mi dwar fool. dwat May.

dwek, dwlk common people. dwi dwi small, black insects in water. dwil, dwill house: (your) dwillu: (their) dwillien. dwil bie, dwil bieni tent. dwil gora or dwil gorka school, dwil jail hotel, inn. academy.

dwilwal clinic; hospital. dwir, dwiri sin; to sin. gwan dwiri, jl dwiri sinner. dwop, dup road; highway; path; (use dup when exact path is mentioned). dwop dier iron bridge. dwop mi gon gon winding road. dwok to dress hair in fashion of another tribe. dwoq, duq shell of ostrich egg. dwoq dancing because happy (used with wedding talk only). dwor, sing, thing; qwak, qwani (plural.) dwoth to relinguish; remainder; bl dwothkien jik to subtract; gur dwothkien to subtract.

dwcth jo k ekuek dwoth jok person who is passed on path. dwoth, dwoth large, black fish. dyeny, dyenyi baby basket; manger. dyok three. dyokdien third.

Dh. dhai sightless. dhal- to astonish; to be dismayed; incomprehensible; impossible. dham dham idle; nonsense. dhar, dhar I jar, large earthern pot. dhar that earthern cooking pot. dher) to bleed; to hemorrhage; nosebleed. dhek dhek throbbing; ticking. dhem bridge between fishtraps. dhie blinded. dhiel to lessen pain; to return to place of; to return with; person who stays in wilderness; one who refuses to quarrel. wal dhiel A sedative, opiate. dhim to squeeze to take water out. dhlai to dissolve.

dhlap to consume; brittle; very old. gwan dhiatni one who boasts of self. dhik dhik sound of footsteps. dhlk- to constantly refuse to help. dhol, dhoii, wic dhula island. dhol to abuse; to despise. dhom to commit adultery. ram ml dhoti not a real man; cie wut pany. dhor to hold tightly because afraid. dhoc entirely full; to lean over in front of; to push or crowd against. dhoal to call you for nothing.

dhol, dholl poss. dhol boy.

dholi gorka, ji gorka students.

dhop leprosy.

ran dhop, ji dhop leper.

dhot- to doubt.

dhual to call to fight.

dhuc pouty person.

dhue to run fast; to jump high.

dhuk kile like turkey beard.

dhuk dhuk (or is it dhok dhok) fat.

dhum adultery.

dhuol to bring bride to home.

dhuor sorry (as when they throw themselves on the ground and cry because of grief). dhuon, dhon small piece of. dhur splash; bang; big ox. dhur gwic rope net left to catch foot of giraffe. dhwor to get away. dhyec five. dhyecdien fifth.

enjel angel.

Ebel Abel.

Ebraam Abraham.

Ebtholum Absalom.

ebuth, yot- ebuth to slap or to hit hard. ecac exactly.

edan one day sometime ago. edhek to spurt out as ce WA edhek (it spurted out). e gik e gik stamping sound made by feet. ejen yes. ekuek at once.

ekuom geka ekuom footsteps.

eh k bang.

elli)- very (when used with full as thiai) eii!)). el or) much; (very) or elurj-eluk with a big slapping sound. erne this. emo that. en same. en I or an I where. enei when. eno so; like this. erja who. erju what.

e ijuan what, same as eiju. e ou e ou jingling. epuc certainly; surely. erac very bad. erau hazy like a mirage. criath when all flee. eric dodged. et et scratching sound; teke et et it has scratching sound. etyat to break in pieces; ce pen etyat it fell in pieces. eterj, entirely finished; ce WA eter) it was entirely finished. ethll absolutely.

ethur to bang with stick as buk ewa they say. ethur.

ewac to revive. ewic entirely; all of them. eyat entirely: finished. eyum entirely: very.

ga verily.

gaac to be amazed; to be astonished; to be surprised.

gak quarrel; to quarrel; vexed; to lock.

gal to throng; to press upon.

gam to sing solo part; to help; to assist; to deliver mother of child; midwife.

gan ganka generations to come; descendants.

gany to prickle as with needles in it.

gany, ganyni land crocodile.

gai) to protect; to guard; to turn; protector; front part of woman's dress made of narrow strips of sheepskin tied together.

gar person who cuts tribal marks; Nuer tribal marks; mark; man.

kwoth mi gar gar omnipresent god.

gat, gaat child; gat mi ka firstborn; gur ka ka second child; gaati dan between second and last child; gat mi gur youngest child now; gat ml pek last child possible.

gat ganka generation; descendant; gaat ganka (pi.).

gat gwani child of father or of uncle.

ci gat kam rar to abort.

gat kwan prince.

gat kel mi cedieth karo only begotten.

gat mi pai dap, gaati ti pai dap infant.

gaum flower; (bud) gaum mi rul.

gal to dally; to halt; to hesitate; stretcher; bier.

gan bed.

gan large grass.

geu eaves; roofing grass.

geugenka cr gegeka to recline.

geka neighboring; nearby; at a little distance; jl geka neighbors.

g (k)ni ge(k)ni on all sides. gel bony; gel (used for man) surrounded. ger comb of hen; to spread apart; to separate; to steer or row a boat; batwing Shullik hairdress. get to bake, to fry. geth- to scrape.

giak to stutter; gikl do you stutter? git to keep punching with spear. git e git to be entirely finished with giek beside. food.

gil persuaded and persuaded; to refuse; to argue; n. ebony. gir hunger. gir to be hungry. giric, gireni piaster. gith to dip out water. go good (pi. of migwaa). goie goodness. gor- to write: gori bakel ke gwath dareu to multiply; n. writing. ji gorka scribes. gok, gokni monkey. gok shell used for ornament; grass, seed of which may be used for food. gok butka scab of sore. gol to pass by; to go around; small smudge fire in barn; home. gol, gwath, poss. golla, gwathni place. jl gol the people of my place; as ji gol IA the people of my place. gon- to hold or carry in hand. goi) blue beads used as headband; to bend; to serve guests with food. gop to remove top part; to take off: to take a crosscut or bypath.

got got to be fidgety as teke got got. goth to stand erect as ce jecde goth he stood erect. gu after while; exactly. gual to go into fire; to sing part song. guan- to beg; to refuse to leave without present, guar, gwath mi la guai) cavern. guar place where roof and walls meet; chest and breast. guat fruitlessly; kept fishing but caught none; to go away on river; to scrape a dish; also a bad word. guath to remove scales from fish. gueny to separate sticks in making fishtrap. guer blessing. gu guk sheltered; gwath mi guguk sheltered place. guk purse; bag; pocket; to retch. guk raven; dove. guk kwoth, gok kwoth prophet. guk nyitni pleural cavity. gul to be surrounded (used for animals); traveler; to go ahead of; wants it also duij gul e. gul- to cool hot water by adding cold. ml gul gul round with hole in center. gule, gulke different. gum not quite full; n. big gourd with small opening in top. gumut, gumuni owl. gun string of bow; n. handle; skunk; civet cat. guny to witness. gunyka n. witness; jl gunyka witnesses. gut) to stoop; ce ro gui) he stooped (himself).

guoce gwath mi Ia tor guocc, guoceni sword.

guok Adam's apple; to shut up; to sew shut. guok stiff, ci yetka guk as my finger is stiff, guol smallpox. guorj, guob guinea fowl. guorj to widen when making fishnet. guot, guotnl insect something like grasshopper but back like big green leaf. gut to reach all the territory it wanted to and to accomplish its purpose. gut pik pouty; to pout. gur spitting snake; to search: to seek: to want; to hunt; to wish. guth act of standing on tiptoe; to take by hand and drag out; side of neck. guwek guwekni spoon. guwek Iwac cartilage at end of breastbone. gwaa pi. tigo good. gwac to make a mistake; to connect; to meet; to pass; n. mistake. gwac- to be cross at each other. gwac A pardon me; I am mistaken. gwacni kc to exchange. g wad in sir. gwak April. gwak oppossum. gwal corral for cattle; to bow; to exchange; to take turns at work; to relieve of burden. gwal ken I rwac debating. gwan father; (my) gwar; (your) gur; (their) gwandicn; (our) gwandan; owner. gwan barjni lucky person.

2 Huffman, Nuer-English gwan bokm librarian.

gwan canya person who is particular about food; one who is prissy. gwan deet, jl deet shepherd. gwan dhomni adulterer. gwan dhota boaster, gwan dor) grandfather. gwandonj ancestors. gwan duothni person who smiles. gwan kac liar.

gwanlen- uncle on father's side. gwan liaka boaster. gwan nyakni unstable person: one who is constantly changing mind. gwan riet mine lawyer. gwan tiela hypocrite: miser: crabbed person. gwan tietka genius. gwan thok interpreter. gwan thu father-in-law. gwan thwokni humble person; truthful person. gwan wal quack doctor; medicine man. gwai) axillary; sound of fish in water. gwap rweini to slobber because talking too fast. gwath com bladder. gwath mi dai stand or high place. gwath kuka store. gwath kwonyka grave. gwath laaka, pi. gwath laakni pasture. gwath mi luij lui) deep place. gwath mi nan nan distant place. gwath mi I a te thin abode. gwath mi thap valley; low place. gwath ml IA tor honeycombed place.

gwathwal gwathwal hospital; clinic.

gwar girl about puberty; to grind.

gwe bark of a dog.

gwec, gwic giraffe.

gwec kwoth prophecy.

gweny to step aside; to make way; to separate; root of lotus, may roast and eat it. gwei) tiep small shrub, used as shield. gwce, gwi gravel. gwek frog.

gwel gwel to talk mixed languages. gwet to attain; to scrape out. gwet gwet to be undecided; locda te gwet gwet my heart is undecided. gwi ice; hail.

gwic to see; to watch; to perceive. gwice gwik to be still hungry. gwi gwic insects, biting cattle before mosquitoes. gwi I to look for; to see; to examine. gwilik small white headed bird. gwir to touch; limit; to comb hair; name of certain village. gwit to rake. gwith pride; stubbornness: proud: warlike; pugnacious. gwith Iwac imagination. gwop skin of person. gwop bum hump on cow. gwop waij eyelid; (upper lid) gwop nhial; lower lid gwop piny, gwok upper part of ear. gwoi) hollowed out; to hew out: to hull; ce jokde g wo I) to be tardy. gwoi), gwoij hedgehog. gwoij cuk flesh on upper part of leg. gwoi person who always goes by self; chase; elephant; rock rabbits; next; to pursue; to follow after. gwoi", gwor mole. gwor ivory armlet. gwori short hair, gwor jail armlet same as made of gourd but made of different thing, very white. Found at

Toe, none at Nasser. gwor ken armlet made of gourd. gwuij to stoop a little; to be bowed over. gwuth- to pick fruit; to pull out hairs.

rei yaa m ne world.

yac, yaC fisherman.

yac to carry on head.

yai to swell up like rice in water.

yam thigh.

yar to spread.

yan en I am here.

yer to urge to take; large container for dura, yoc to be damp; to be wet; to warm body, yoie pelvic region; hip; lumbar vertebrae. yom trap as hole dug to catch animals.

yor to revive; to restore; n. restorer, yok to push. yok cattle (pi.) of yai)-yol roofing grass. yon help me; tc try.

voir jen badak yon to test; to measure.

yor ambatch.

yui to crawl on hands and feet with back next to ground. yuk gourd with hole in top. yunh to return from journey. yur cupping to get blood out, small cuts are made and then place cow horn over cut and suck on it to get blood out. yut, yutni shelf; ledge. yuth propeller; to journey.

I that.

id I how.

le whether.

imei fishing season ahead.

imith which.

in-, tin- prefixes specifying particular; the.

in in which.

mbor, tinbor the white.

indan the thing that we were.

inene like this.

I no thus.

mono the same.

intot, tintot the small.

irun tomorrow; sometime in future; indefinite time ahead.

ithiaij this afternoon.

lyo afterwhile.

ja it; him; her.

jac to reach; nhial to look up, to shoot, (when thing shot at is hit). 2 jacni first came to. as jacni Gwir first came to Gwir. jaia to want to leave, 1st. pers. sing. jai ni jc to deny (falsely). jakok crow; mirol crow with white throat. jak pany top of wall. jal nausea; to belch. jal to walk; to journey; visitor; WA to rinse: a math to walk slowly; jor to overflow: ke mal to crawl; ke jok jok to walk backwards; thok yiir to wade in water at river bank; ibis; guest; visitor. jalab, jalabni arab merchant. jalany bran soaked in water and soured. jany shallow; to prolong; to dally; to delay. jai) to take. jaij, jaai) servant. jath to be sorry; sorrow as ci locda jath am sorry. jath, jen; poss. jiath, jien tree; jath dun, yar also called jath yai) is a certain club. jak to jump up and down; to shake; to churn; to send a person. JAr, JAN shoulder. jec to scrape the black off. jec, poss. jic abdomen; stomach; inside. je her; him; it.

jec to stand up; nhial to lift up. jen he; she; it. jen badak eighty. jen badak wicde kel eighty-one. jen badak wicde reu eighty-two. jen badak wicde dyok eighty-three.

jen badak wicde ijwan jeth en badak wicde ijwan eighty-four.

en badak wicde dhyec eighty-five.

en badak wicde bakel eighty-six.

en badak wicde baro eighty-seven.

en badak wicde badak eighty-eight.

en badak wicde baijwan eighty-nine.

en bakel sixty.

en bakel wicde kel sixty-one.

en bakel wicde reu sixty-two.

en bakel wicde dyok sixty-three.

en bakel wicde ijwan sixty-four.

en bakel wicde dhyec sixty-five.

en bakel wicde bakel sixty-six.

en bakel wicde baro sixty-seven.

en bakel wicde badak sixty-eight.

en bakel wicde baijwan sixty-nine.

en baijwan ninety.

en baijwan wicde kel ninety-one.

en baijwan wicde reu ninety-two.

en barjwan wicde dyok ninety-three.

en baijwan wicde ijwan ninety-four.

en baijwan wicde dhyec ninety-five.

en baijwan wicde bakel ninety-six.

en baijwan wicde baro ninety-seven.

en baijwan wicde badak ninety-eight. jen baijwan wicde baijwan ninety-nine. jen baro seventy. jen baro wicde kel seventy-one. jen baro wicde reu seventy-two. jen baro wicde dyok seventy-three. jen baro wicde ijwan seventy-four. jen baro wicde dhyec seventy-five. jen baro wicde bakel seventy-six. jen baro wicde baro seventy-seven. jen baro wicde badak seventy-eight. jen baro wicde baijwan seventy-nine. jen dhyec fifty. jen dhyec wicde kel fifty-one.

en dhyec wicde reu fifty-two. en dhyec wicde dyok fifty-three. en dhyec wicde ijwan fifty-four. en dhyec wicde dhyec fifty-five. en dhyec wicde bakel fifty-six. en dhyec wicde baro fifty-seven. en dhyec wicde badak fifty-eight. en dhyec wicde baijwan fifty-nine. en dyok thirty. en dyok wicde kel thirty one. en dyok wicde reu thirty two. en dyok wicde dyok thirty three. en dyok wicde ijwan thirty four, en dyok wicde dhyec thirty five. en dyok wicde bakel thirty six. en dyok wicde baro thirty seven. en dyok wicde badak thirty eight. en dyek wicde baijwan thirty nine. ene it is here. en ijwan forty. en ijwan wicde kel forty-one. en ijwan wicde reu forty-two. en ijwan wicde dyok forty-three. en ijwan wicde ijwan forty-four. en ijwan wicde dhyec forty-five. en ijwan wicde bakel forty-six. en ijwan wicde baro forty-seven. en ijwan wicde badak forty-eight. en ijwan wicde barjwan forty-nine. ereu twenty.

ereu wicde kel twenty-one. ereu wicde reu twenty-two. ereu wicde dyok twenty-three. ereu wicde ijwan twenty-four. ereu wicde dhyec twenty-five. ereu wicde bakel twenty-six. ereu wicde baro twenty-seven. ereu wicde badak twenty-eight. ereu wicde baijwan twenty-nine. eth to wade across; to cross over.

juok- ji clatter; noise.

jiai the people, of.

jie to sting as when hand touches ice.

jier lime.

jith to stop raining.

jiu, jiuni, poss. jio well.

jl, ye you.

jl geka neighbors.

jllth scorpion.

dui) jic, nym jic abdominal.

jiec immediately.

jlk to find.

jl ke people; relations.

j 11 chaff.

jin, yen (nom. form); jl, ye (objective) you. jin to lie down: to rest; to lie awake.

jli) thui strong grass used for fishline. jipni altogether. jl tietka yaa prophets. jlth ear. jlth leaf. jlth Iwac auricle. jo voice; sound. jom wind; season of cool winds; to dip out. jo I) to forget for a minute. jony itches; to scratch; n. juny. jop to fell; to chop. jop to shrink, ci ro jop it shrunk itself, ba joe I will see about it (used in 1st person only). tet joe crippled (without one hand). joe to be stranded; somewhat dry but not entirely. jok bones of cervical region; back (poss. jok); surely; behind; certainly; ghost; of a truth; cattle and sheep disease but they are different. jok, jokni week. ce ben ka jok tardy. jok wee back of village. jol in succession. joi) to lie down ce rode jorj as he laid himself down. jor (ajor) absent; to be lost; outside; to run outside alone. jot kel one pound Egyptian; ten. juak measles.

juak udder; one kind of red dura. jual tail, juan (bi ci ro juan) to wrinkle; (the cloth wrinkled itself). juat feather; kot- feather fan. judol red and white ox. juik aluminum hearts made to wear around waist. juk thuom crossbar of fiddle. juk thill k, juk thillkni bicycle. juk (mtot) dog; (indit) horse. juk- to plaster part way up wall (CA juk ke cement). juk lee fish that bites. juk mwon top (toy for children). juk nyapec coyote; wild horse. Jul only living child; one kind of fish. Jul certain headdress for woman, 4 turfs of hair left on head to show she has but one child. Jul A to pick a quarrel. jum cheek; jawbone. juntoc black and white ox with green head (extinct now). juoc to chase; to run off. riem be juoc to bruise. juok- to jump in (cike ro juokni yir) they jumped in river).

juok cuka kapeni juok cuka metatarsal.

juol, jol hip joint.

jup, jupni ax.

jur, juri sore coming without any cause seemingly and disappearing similiarly. jurr, jurr foreignor. jut to annoy; to urge persistently; to tease; to pester. jut, juit old maid. juth Jews; ran Juth, ji Juth Jew. juk- to say; to reply. jur) very hot water but not boiling. jur), jur) a very high platform; rack for dura heads; shelter for dura. jwac, rei jwa(c)ni grass; rei juol in certain kind of grass. ram mi jwar grasping. jwath one kind of fish. jwath tet, jwath tetni forearm. jwe, jwath poss. jwathni sickness; disease, illness; jl jwathni the sick people. jwir grasping. jwot long stick with ambatch head that is carried by newly gar- ed boys. jyarj- to skin animal. jyek bad; dirty; (Iwac) mad; a locdu CI jyek cheer up; jyek e jyek very bad; gwan jyekni, ji jyekni devil; demon; jyek erac very bad.

ka or; but: to.

kaam gateway or passageway.

kac to sting; to pinch one's body between wood; to lie; to deny; to bite; n. lie. ml kac kac bitey (like peppers). kac-nhlam to pass another on path, kac piny to alight; to step down; to hop. kac riem artery. kai satisfied (used with water only); to quench thirst. kak, kak, poss. rei kaka, rei kakni field; farm. kak to hunt.

kal, kaal fence; wall around yard. kal kal small skin for rug; hot water bottle. kal Iwac fatty covering of heart. kam between. kam pamni valley. kam puothni ke nyiet pleural cavity. kam ral cartilage. kan to appropriate; to escape; to save; to take; to steal; to go inside. kan, kenne used with negative; not. kan Saviour. kany to rise; rising. kany car) east. kany dwil to come in. kany- to want to take hold. kany i)uok north winds; winter season. kany rar to jump in or down. kai) kwar, kai) kwari kingfisher. kai) to deceive; to fool. kar) cornet; whistle: mouth organ; bugle. kap forceps; pliers; thong. kap(de) tail of fish. kapeni shaking dura to get fine out; to sift.

kap tick kap tick sing, kapni tick pi. hinge.

kap rac n. catch (of fish).

kap yie, kap yieni food which may be eaten raw while awaiting cooked food. kar branch or bough of tree; to cut in long strips as cutting meat. kar A, karo; karo I only; only; they only. kat, kat bird like hawk. kat, katnl sleeping place for women in fishing camp. kat A meat and mush eaten together but cooked separately; salt. kat kat to be very sharp teke kat kat. katipe vegetable like potato. cyek mi kau, man ti kath bride; newly married woman. ka, ke seed and fiber in gourd; pulp. kak reputation; report; to cleai one's throat; to split. kak to spread apart as ce cukke kak piny he spread his feet apart. kal to court a girl; ce WA kal he went courting. kalam Nuer hoe. kam to give (when one must walk to get it, use kam; when hand it use nun,). kal moon. kap to catch; to take hold of; to transplant. el piny kap calm. karakon jail; prison. kar kar, kar kaN spider; web. kat kite. kath bile; breast of cow; rust; mold; to stumble on (ca cukda nak ke kath); gallbladder.

ke path between neighbors.

kea certain herb.

kec to be angry; quarrel which started with play.

keel to urge to go.

kec I ka to call off dog; big talk; loud.

keliu all.

keu reedbuck; bushbuck; chest.

key A certain grass, women eat it cooked, young men refuse it, old men eat it.

ke with; and; from; them.

keac wooden beads.

keac, kec dura birds.

kedl how many.

kek to draw lines on paper: to scratch (ce ya kek) it scratched me.

kek, kekni, poss. kik dike.

kel one.

keloi), keloijni squash; pumpkin.

ken, kan, ci not; sign of negative.

ken they.

kendial all of them.

kendial ewic every one of them.

kene and.

kenke sign of negative pi. not.

ker to awaken; to scratch on ground as bith mi ker ran piny fishing spear which one scratches on ground; to cut little cuts on body to let blood out; nail worn in upper lip of Nuer girl and in lower lip of Anuak girl.

ker foundation of house.

ker, ken gourd.

ker ker, ker ken lizard.

kerui)wan morning; in the morning.

ket burnt work on gourd.

ket to swim; to sing; to shake rattle kete kuak to quiet child; club; bird with long, red legs, white breast, brown back; walking stick (pi.

ketni). kete surely; now. to laud. keteth red peppers, also called ml mit. keue to declare (falsely); to ask emphatically is it I? kick (ca wicda kick juat) to put ornament in or on head; put feather on my head, kieldokral bird with beard, long legs. kien egrets. kicr certain kind of club; name of tree; loss of appetite today; when rainy season wants to start. kil saddle billed jaribu; maribou. kirn, kimni doctor; physician.

kir to bloat; gas rumbling in bowels (ci jecda kir). kit ke tok to laugh heartily. kle or.-klcn pi. suffix meaning theirs; sing.

-dien. klk scratch, kll, kill rhinoceros. kin I incessantly; repeatedly. kir, kin, poss. klir river. kite finally. kith cow urine. kith to sprinkle; to sow; to plant corn, koc cold; to sew: to mend; weak as koc c te. kocdlcn the first of them. kok to ache. kom to husk; to thrash. kom, kuam worm.

kom yak A mushroom shaped thing that gtows in ground, not eaten.

kop (Ia dwopde e kope), as mole makes hole.

kok, gwath koka grave.

kok all broken up ci rol kok keliu all the country broken up or destroyed; to buy; to sell; to barter; to be stranded; to trade; to be kind; to comfort.

kokien pi. of dodlen others.

kol to dodge; to fan; tallow; horsetail used as fan.

kom, komni chair; Nuer pillow for men.

kom bie, kom bieni our kind of pillow.

kon, (nom.), ko (obj.) we.

kon; kone first.

kondial kel all of us together.

kone I and.

koij to welcome; to hasten to; big noise.

kop to distend as balloon blown up; to be swollen, used for ground and dead animals; certain grass along river.

kop mush.

kor, kur war.

kor after; behind.

kor qaii), kori big fight between tribes.

kot to hang up; to climb; vine with thorns.

kot nhial to fly.

koth to fertilize.

ku seems to express habitual action.

-ku,-kun suffix meaning yours.

kuak trap for animals.

kuak kwan kwan kuak to grab unexpectedly; kap kuak to grab when they are not expecting it. kual, kual calf. kuaq intoxicating drink. kuat to hide.

kuath to tie together with grass. kuc n. sewing; to restore. kuit, kui(t)ni ivory armlet. kuk kindness: to utter a series of short sounds. kuk, poss. kuka hole as hole in tree. kuk kwoth sacrifice. kul skin to sleep or sit on; Nuer bed; disease which draws one's body together. ku lo nien a gwaa (sing.) goodby; kwa lo nien a gwaa (pi.) goodby (when bidding several goodby). kul yo metal rug. kum husk of corn; eggshell; pod; to overshadow. kum, kumni hat; lid; cover. kum jiath bark of tree. kumekumto keep hitting; sound of sticks as they hit fish. kum lai) steel helmet. kun, kwoan pi. poss. kwoanni rat. kul) n. race; to race. kuoc buffalo that goes off by itself; to run off by oneself. ram mi kuoc stingy man; miser; hermit. kuom grunt; to cast a shadow. kuon to refuse to eat with one because they have quarrelled, ci mith kuon. kuot fattened. kuok to be faint from hunger; to die of hunger.

kuoth marrow.
kup kupni mush well cooked.
kur cleaver; finger joints; to scratch nose. ram mi kur proficient or clever person.
ran kur, nei tl kur warrior, kurrien their war. kur daf) reu two hundred; kur dyok
three hundred; kur darj ijwan four hundred; kur darj dhyec five hundred. kur 11
bath dor all large numbers. kurum crunch. kut, kuni shield; step; cane along river;
place of the buffalo. kut beside; dry. kut kut, kut ku(t)ni colt; pup. kuth tall grass
in swamp; reed. kuth midit swampy. kwa little, scant. ml kwa car erne sometime
soon. kwac kwac soft. kwac, kwacni leopard. kwac yir kingfisher. kwac spotted; to
scratch: to sharpen, used for pointing big things, not used for pencils; to dig out roots
of trees; bead, oblong, thin, many colored, worn singly; fin. kwai seeds for planting
as seedcorn. kwak sore which persistently stays bad ram mi teke kwak (person who
has persistent sore). kwaka, pi. of twok dishes. kwal to steal. kwal tot finger or toe
nail. ke kwal stealthily; secretly. kwallan, kwallani one kind of bird, kwan kwan,
kwan kwannilobeofear.

kwany kwith kwal kwany to pick up; to collect; to gather; to rake. kwany cuk to
learn to walk as baby does. kwany kwany to walk carefully. kwanywalthwan Nasser.
kwaqle to float or to swim on back. kwar, kwaar chief. kwat small pimples on neck
where hair is shaved. kwal part of husk of dura. kwar to gather. kwat, kwatni nerve
of body. kwe, kwith fishing eagle (or is it stork). kwe bot bot cuckoo. kwec-, do not
know kwac-, l 9t pers.

sing; kwic- is also used in 3d.

pers. kwec to hoe grass; to hoe ground when no rain as yet. kwer to wrestle, kwir
is one form. kwer no grass. kwe wanting to return. kwek to husk; to hull; to peel.
kwel to be spongy. kwel a yok certain constellation of stars. yaq mi kwelita cow,
brown body, white head. kwem disease something like yaws. kwen to wear upper
and lower bracelets; to count; to find; (amath) talk slowly; (jo) read aloud; ci nhiemde
kwen to bind hair on account of sorrow. kwen to marry. kwen food. kwen ku nyuor
when wedding talk kwendek dropsy.

kwen, trot.
kwet, kwet tortoise; turtle.
kwet to kick.
kwet calf that is weaned.
kwi for; small elephant; why.

ram mi kwi mithde one who eats little. kwic side; yonder; across. kwicimi opposite
side, kwiel small hiding place. kwieny (pi bi kwieny pwonyde) to run off as water
when body is greased (water will run off his kwik eagle. body).

kwiny to toss about; to move about; to bully; to torment; to pick up with hand.
kwiny kwiny fussy; ashamed (teke kwiny kwiny). kwinyuot June. kwiye, kwike few;
scant; too small; too young. kwi a smaller.

kwi I, kwel hole in anything: star. kwil stealing. kwi IA yuk little dipper. kwil
Clke ro luai certain constellation of stars. kwil le jok milky way. kwin marriage.

kwir to fall; threw spear at him. kwir kec to wrestle until they are mad. kwit male
lamb. kwit- v. beating of heart; n. heart beat. kwith to curse; n. curse. kwith kwal
(ram mi kwith kwal) one brave about hunger.

kwoan kwoan (ce kwoan) to be mad, (he was mad).

kwoc, kwoc instep.

kwom to cover up; (piny) to cover.

kwony (can) setting sun; to bury.

kwor, kur hundred.

kwor kel one hundred; kwor kel wicde kel one hundred one; kwor kel wicde reu one hundred two; kwor kel wicde dyok one hundred three; kwor kel wicde wal one hundred ten; kwor kel wicde wal wicde kel one hundred eleven; kwor kel wicde jereu one hundred twenty; kwor kel wicde jereu wicde reu one hundred twenty two.

kwoth a small fish; to snort; to whistle as ci ryei kan. kwoth; as the boat blew whistle.

cak kwoth monstrosity.

kwoth, kuth God.

kwok, kwi, poss. pi. kwini thorn; fork.

kwok must; to force one to; occiput.

kwol wristlet of black and white beads worn by man whose wife is pregnant to protect him from sores and cuts.

kwor joint of finger.

kwore piny to count age less than it is.

kwot to adorn body in order to attract one of opposite sex.

kwot, kwotnl ardeb tree.

kwut, kwuni suitor.

labith, labitheni fishhook. lac to defecate; menses.

lajok one class of Nuers; (of long ago, all dead now). lak to graze; to wash; to slobber; to foam at mouth. bl wicde lak ke pi kwoth to baptize. lak lak e ke to dream. lal- to pierce.

lam to curse: to imprecate. lamba lamp; candle. Ian Ian very good. lany to put ashes on hair to bleach it. laij lai), poss. Ian laqni swing. laijerep, larjerepni Sudani bed. lap rice. lapa adv. like. lap a bitl to be still and refuse to talk. lar to tell; to say; to go slowly. lar lar to go to tell the news. I at work; job; to work; to speak. lat e wicde karo to support, literally, (work is on his head only). lat ke lat to visit. lat mi bee bee hard work. lat- luar working for pleasure. lat- riak working for necessities of life. lath to put; to call; to entice; to tremble; to put on airs; affected. lath corns as on feet. lath ken soldiers. lath- lieth wic- to anoint. lath puk to sift ashes. lau- one section of Nuerland. laue of soft consistency like prepared mustard. IA always;-I A suffix meaning my, used with nowns ending in 1.

-lien I At) to request; to beseech; to petition; brass bracelets; ring; bald. lap to be very hot as sun is hot; v. to lap. lat, let, poss. leet, leni orge. I At comb. lee, lee tooth. lecke nyieny to make a face when eating something bitter, lei, lei, poss. leini wild animal. lek- to shut. lek, poss. lek certain large fish, delicious. I eke to ruminate. te lek lek to rock. lei- to eat; to do; to make. thlle ml lei it makes no difference. leni repeatedly. lenye, lenyke comparative form; exceeding; surpassing. leu tuber resembling potato. leu, leuni oar; bamboo. le repeatedly but not always; again; -le suffix meaning its, hers, his used with nouns ending in 1. lem lem to go a little ways, stop, then go on; te lem lem. lei) almost fell. Icp to open. lep, leep tongue. Icp lep strips: shreds; to eat skin that is blistered. lep tot fangs of snake. ler to roll; awhile. lerke slowly.

let, poss. leet waist; dorsal vertebrae. leth perspiration; hot. lia, poss. Math death. Mac dried fish.

Mac pregnant, used with cattle. liak to praise; to commend; to praise with words; (ro) to boast.

n. praise. gwan Maka, ji Maka boaster; hypocrite. Mam to mix; to spy out; to mingle with. Mai)- to open mouth forcibly. IJAk oesophagus. liak to tickle. Mai to peek at when provoked; to peer. lide kel same form. lieny harpoon used by Anuaks to kill hippos. lieny kwoth judgment of God. Mel, liell stream; tributary of river. Mel jok backbone. lier- to cut. Met (ci pi Met A cika gwi) to freeze, the water froze when it became ice. Meth grease of any kind; fat; oil; place to tie cattle. lik heart throbbing (ci loeda WA lik) my heart throbbed. Ml- to drink all of it; to empty; to drain. liny, linyni flea. lip-, to wait. 2nd. person, sing.

Mpni, 2nd. person, plural liape. lip nyal fiance. liu to perish; to die.

I lap to mix together.

Iiap hap to blink as teke hap hap he is blinking.

Il ail chronic illness.

-hen suffix added to nouns ending in 1, meaning theirs.

tuck llercni class of Nuers whose tribal marks were out in 1926. Ilet, poss. Iltka sand. Mm to beg; when cold winds start and then warm weather comes lime sweet. again.

Iim Mm delicious. liny to sort out.

Ill) to throw down as in wrestling. Ill)- to hear. WA III) entirely full. line ka biete dumb but not deaf. lip fishing bird. Mr scrofula. lire to melt. Iith (biel mi lith) tan. Iithgaac intot, hthgaac indit classes of Nuers. The Iithgaac intot is about 20 to 25 years old now.

The Iithgaac indit is about 25 or 26 years old now. lo afterwards. lok trigger of gun; belt of cane stalks worn by newly gar- ed boys. lony to loosen; to untie. lony poss. luony lion. lop to cock; to put food on fire to cook. lou big water animal much feared (now extinct, possibly mythical) lou white hair. loc luc, poss. Iwac, lucni heart; ventricle. loc cuk center of sole of foot; loc tet center of palm of hand, locdaa hearts of all of us. loip- fever; to be feverish. lok to blow away. loki tramp.

lok lok when food is cooking and spatters out of pot; teke lok lok. lokothiai, lokothiaieni mosquito net. lol to take out; to pluck out; place where the river is deep. loi)- to rest. loi) gut crooked staff. loi) ro never mind, lop placenta. lor- to go to meet. lore empty; naked. lorke to sacrifice. lot heart beat. loth cotton; thread. lotkero to follow after. lok- to refuse; n. refusal; ci ro lok to commit suicide; ce lok eloi) to abhor; lok-to search; to go to one place and then another.-lu,-lun suffix for nouns (ending in 1), meaning yours. lua to always come when person is absent. luac gum of tree; wax. Iliac luac spongy. luai to file in; to lower (may also use lue piny), luak, luek barn. lual skinned place that hurts. lualdit poisonous snake, red, also called rir. luai), luai) fly. luai) luai) to stroll slowly. luar to recede. luc, luc cattle stakes. luc to change mind; to return from; elevated; n. sterile (man). luc ke thok to translate. luek to admonish; to reason with; to reprove; n. peacemaker.

luck luck, lulk discipline.

luel to exchange; to replace.

luei) to assent; to poison: n. poison.

lull to exchange things of equal value. luk to hunt; to spread; n. navel. luk locdu ke ya forgive me. luk luk tadpoles. lukni- to go along river instead of across. lul cry.

lum prayer; lover; to court, lundur machine gun. lunkur wrigley. luny to return. luny bi pwonydu put your clothes on; to dress. luny- loc to forgive; to have mercy. luny nhial fish that falls with rain, luny (or) luony to leak. luny thieni moles. luny wicde jor to overflow. lui) tuber like potato, requires much cooking. lui) ro stand on your head. lui) artificial respiration; deep. lui) lui) steep. luoce to repeat.

luoc luoc higher slope, not a hill. luoi, nei ti luoini person who cannot swim, luoke to fly over. luom courtship; small dance; news of dance; to slander. luor tree with red trunk, thorny; to be tied loosely. luot to be afraid; impregnation when child is not weaned; muscles of back; abscess; east; west; length.

CA ro luot they match.

CI ro luot piny as snake going in hole.

luot to be partly cooked.

luoth early morning.

lut to impregnate when child is nursing as ce gat lut. lut to advance head down; to put head to ground; to belch. luth elephant trunk. luth fish that stays in swamp or dry land, makes cacoon. luth- to tell bad. luthrun morning rain. Iutke(nyure lutke) to be idle; unused. luth, luth bell. luAk to help. lui) to call.

Iwak, Iwek snail; mussel; oyster. Iwany to soak.

Iwai), ci locde ku Iwai) to be happy. Iwai) to help; help; aid; able. Iwei) deep.

Iwceth to suckle ci man gat Iwccth. Iweth gat cc man Iweth to nurse. Iwilwi, Iwilwini duck. Iyec to look upward.

ma(r) mother, directly addressed. maath pl. maathni friend; friendship maathdien. mac fire.

mac gun; labor pains; to cheat. mac din shotgun.

do mac, de mac shell for gun; n. shot. mad in title for older woman, addressed directly. madhieth bladder. mai to fish.

mai tela mai tei A to fish by wading in swamps.

mal greeting; easy; light; peaceful; welcome.

male sound; in good shape; safe.

mall, malu, male direct greeting hail.

mam to hit.

mamero to change mind right now.

man, poss. mani mother; women (pi. only as cyek is singular form).

mandoi), mardoi) grandmother; my grandmother.

man ganke daughter-in-law.

mani and.

man l car kel never.

mani jak never.

mani pai I co lee never (emphatically) used when there is great famine.

manlieth, manhethni hawk.

man palek, man pale(k)ni hen; chicken.

manyan, honored surname among Nuers for girls.

manytap, manytapni maize; corn.

mai), poss. maijka wave.

mar, mor my mother; your mother.

mar friendship.

thile ke mar, duqdien gak what we call jealousy among men (literally, they no friendship, belonging to them quarrel).

mar- to guess; to speak false rumors marak to call with loud voice tc place where fish are found.

mare family of brothers and sisters.

mar man riddle; trick.

mar nhial thunder; lightning.

marthu, morthu, manthu my mother- in- law; your mother-in-law; mother-in-law. mat to fold; to multiply; to add. math to reconcile as math nei ro; we reconcile ourselves. math to drink. math to absorb; to ally with; whisper. mathol onion. ma slang kid, used by men only. mat to go outside and afterwhile return. me introducing time clause of completed action. mei poss. mai fishing season. me; ml if. meat n. plot, meedan sometime ago. meepan yesterday. meepan ke caqdar yesterday noon. mek- to choose. mekana machine gun; engine; sewing machine; typewriter. nicker one class of Nuers, now about 50 55 years old. me me this. men to weave as a fishnet; to turn as winding road; bl candle WA men to put top on. mepethlth district commissioner. mer to opine that it surely did look like; to lighten as with lamp; to stay absent; tears; vitreous humor; light. mer mer dazzling. merun the next day. met to taste; to plot; to deceive; to fool; to beguile. met never; anus.

mewalka mewalka, mewmka, mcwin, mewal long ago. mi giraffe hair. miak, miakni insect always biting animals. mien to pinch; to slam ci thok dwil ro mien; the door of the house slammed (itself). miei) deaf, dumb or both, n. mir). mier ya. sunset. miet to catch hand in door; to tread on each other; to shut as mi (et) ni yetku; shut your hand; ca thukkien miet their mouths were shut. mile glutted; satiated. mim charcoal.

min min muscles of upper arm. miot, mioni hoof. mit, mieni fireworm. mit, mit firefly. mit rainbow. mith food; to eat. mi which; introducing relative clause. mi bar, or mi bar bar tall; very tall. mibor, tibor white. micor, ticur blind. midit, tidit; big. midul red. milual, tilual red. ml mi this (when thing is at a little distance). m I n since; when; to fight very much. mmdan awhile ago. mingul why. mm war last night. minwarui) this morning. minyai) brown. mil) to sorrow.

mir to remember; to hit, same as juac. mir to refuse to lend to friend. au mir evening; WA mir to go at sunset. miric government. mir mir faintly. mirnyin head band of beads. mit, mm mini big limb of tree. mit smudge fire in barn; fireplace in barn. mit to snap fingers. mitath big (used with spear only). mi thar last year. mi thar ke je year before last. mi tlth red. mi toe green; yellow. mi toe yil green. mi yil blue. mi yil car brown. ml yil lual seal brown. mi yil liet purple. mi wal mei last fishing season. mo sign of emphatic action. moc to give; to sting ci pien e moc. moc, muc n. gift. moc-pwony ke bi to dress. mom piny unexpectedly; surprised.

mok to rise as river rises. mola day after tomorrow. mola dodlen day after day after tomorrow, molthin to cover over, mo mo that. mon, to visit; visit. gwath mon, k A visiting room or space, mony to blow and spit on one when greeting one; also a work of t he medicine man. mor to massage with hot water.

nei ni dial mor eastern part of Lau country, opposite section called Guny. mor mor certain kind of large ant. mot to be faint. moth secretly; plot. mdk buffalo. muac to mention name of one's pet steer when praising; to call loudly. muany- to husk by rolling grain in hands. ram mi muc generous person. mill carbuncle; boil; cartilage. mul, mull mule. mum, muomni roan antelope. mun, poss. mwon dirt; ground. muom to run away ci jin e muom you ran away. muoc to spatter out of kettle; to splash. muok part of fish that is bad. muol, mual knee. muol to cover as cover seeds with ground; to press dirt over seed with foot. muol muol gentle. muor to slumber lightly. muot sightless; blind. muot A coi very sharp. muoth- to sharpen; to bite hard food as toast; to gnaw. muoth atlth to eat but not finish meal; to eat raw food. rei muoth in the darkness. murkir tail of gourd. mut, muni spear. mut name of Nuer god; blinded; to splice; to sacrifice on account of death of person; to leave off mourning; to shave; something 3 Huffman, Nuer-English about menstruation; sexual intercourse.

muth dark of moon.

mual to crawl.

muAm to swallow as fish does bait.

muath muath silently; to whisper.

muk to reverse as ci ro muk jok it reversed itself.

mul, mull enlarged knee.

mum to eat; small pieces.

muon to faint mwaa to drown.

mwon grave.

nac cow which has not yet calved.

nai to wrap around; to twine around.

naiwal vine.

nak n. death; to kill.

nam to accompany.

nai) to take away.

nar uncle on mother's side.

nar mwon fishworm.

nath people.

naye- to climb as a vine.

nak sour milk; buttermilk; to eat; shelf; to be entirely finished with food as ce nak piny.

nana far.

nan nan at a distance.

napec disease of cattle and sheep.

nedial, nadial everybody; all the people.

neeke his people; disciples.

nei, na people.

nei when.

nei ni dial all of the people.

nhir-rwac nei tl bor white people; Caucasians.

nei tl dit adults.

nei tl luek, helpers; partners; nei tl lue(k)ni helpers; partners.

nei ti nath Nuers.

nei tl wal people of long ago.

nei tl yani yellow people.

nenike descendants; generations yet to come.

ner to salute.

ncn to see.

ncn, nenni mirror.

nie din dim immediately; now.

nien sleep; to sleep.

nicn ke wil interrupted sleep.

ci nicnu, nicn gaatku a gwaa greetings do you sleep well; are your children well.

nict wax in ear; dirt which collects on bodv; rust.

nie tame pany immediately; now.

nieth to be senseless; obstinate; wrong.

nin nights; to pass the time.

nil) very narrow; when one is smaller or undeveloped as CI cuk Nyapini nirj (the foot of Nyapini is undeveloped or smaller).

noc- to sweep up dirt in dustpan.

no mm bel when dura is very fine.

nompiny- class of Nuers of long ago all dead now.

nor- to bring.

nor Old Nasser.

nor- to pound it fine; to bruise.

nok epilepsy.

nuai meat and mush cooked together.

nil an quite dirty; very bad.

nuanc tough as meat is tough.

nuai) palsy.

nuar certain kind of white dura.

nuat life.

nuan thin.

nuer- v. people of murdered person never eat with relatives of murderer.

nuir to never die; to live forever.

nuk to fish with fishing spear.

nuk, nukm blue heron.

nuoi) to travel, same as uth.

nuor to fall to pieces; tender.

nuor; nuon tired.

nuor- to kill.

nuor, nur trunk of dom palm.

nup flour; finely pounded dura.

nup to invite; to send word.

nhial heaven; sky; up.

ran nhial, ji nhial angel.

ci nhial dam to rain.

nhial gil a dam to rain steadily.

nhial ci mar to thunder and lightning.

CI nhial ijok rainy season stopped.

nhiam face; forward; in front of; east; west.

nhian well nourished.

nhiem hair.

nhiem pieth short hair; bobbed hair.

nhiem thok mustache; whiskers.

nhir, nhir water tortoise.

nhir- lat perfect work; no mistakes; correct.

nhir-rwac perfect words; no mistakes; correct.

nhit nhlt to use a cane.

nhok to agree; to be willing; to acquiesce; to be satisfied. nhok to love; to assent. nhok n. love; assent; order.

nyaal python.

nyac harvesting season; teke nyac; to have but little vision.

nyak to throw away something you are very fond of; to take away; n. jealousy, used with women only.

nyakai) poisonous snake.

nyak war, daughter of chief; princess.

nyal, nyier girl.

nyal can girl who has never developed and cannot bear children.

nyal co sterile woman.

nyaleci ual certain kind of white dura.

nyalotkwok certain kind of white dura.

nyal lual variegated red.

nyal pam daughter of mountain.

nyal pini slime on top of water.

nyam, nyier; nyiti (directly addressed), girl.

nyam mi dik dik nice girl.

nyam mi rier rier flirt.

nya nyade, nya gatde girl grandchild.

nya nyiman, nya deman niece.

nyan testicles.

nyancek certain kind of white dura.

nyai) to be saturated; soaked; to wallow in; brown.

nyai), nyur) crocodile.

nyaijgeri spears used by Anuaks to pay for wives.

nyar gum of mouth.

nyawuthgul certain red dura, very tall. nyeu, nyeuni cat.

nyeth to imitate; to mock; to echo. nyiam lower front teeth which Nuers take out. nyieny- mad; fighting. nyim fins.

nyith, nyith mosquito. nyier dwil gcrka schoolgirls. nyier tl jiet fully developed girls. nyik, nyikni the fellow wife. nyikarj certain kind of white dura. nyiman, nyimani sister; (my) nyimar; (your) nyimor. nyin property; belongings. nym jala baggage. le nym nathi where is your faith? nyin yar name of yellow cow. nyipatl certain kind of white dura, nyir n. hate; to hate. nyireu certain kind of white dura. nyith to try. nyith person who has all they need but is continually asking for more. nyith nyith naughty. nyoc flood.

nyor to warm a portion of body. nyok to repeat. nyok, nyok louse. nyok ke lep to reopen. nyole to cry repeatedly. nyai) to climb or twine as vine. nyop- to knead; to mix. nyop to be lazy; (ram mi) lazy person. nyot to stir; to mix. mi nyu nyu small, like small writing.

nyuac i)er nyuac to long for.

nyuak to eat roasted part of partly roasted fish; man who will inherit wife; one who eats with you. mi nyuany to have teeth as fish spear. nyuany gau cameleon. nyuani white beads. nyuat name of tree used for splicing injured rib. nyuar sprinkle of rain, nyuen straw. nyuen en in to stampede. nyuen, nyueni spiked bracelet. nyueny animal somewhat like land crocodile. nyuer to notch ornaments. nyuer, nyueer raindrop. nyuit to touch in passing. nyuk cud. nyurj- to strain intoxicating drink thru bag. nyungul buzzard. nyuon to wrinkle up. nyuoi), also nyuij to wrap around; to tie. nyuony disease somewhat like yaws. nyuoth- to show; to point out. nyuothka n. showing. nyur- to sit. nyur- amath peaceful. nyur mul mull to knell. nyur ke nyurrien to sit quietly as they sit quietly cike nyur ke nyurrien. nyum nyum, nyum nyumni cannibal, nywei to chew; to masticate.

l-ija, eija who.

ijaac to milk.

ijaac del female lamb.

qac to know.

i)ac momo ke Iwacdu do you believe that?

rjak man! (exclamation).

i)ak nom to argue; to contradict.

I)ale large bracelet; thin wristlet; wristlet with two prongs.

i)am to open as open mouth; to yawn; to cook dura whole without pounding ci bel rjam.

n, ai) to growl as dog growls; to fool one.

nap to hang up.

nap ro ke dhot. qap ro ke dhotni bat.

ijar to play; sour; all very sorry; artery in neck throbbing; game.

ijar rjar crying, almost in tears.

came ijar i)ar thokda something invisible bites my mouth.

Ijat to peel; oblong, thin, white bead, worn singly.

ijath trust; to trust; ijath ke Iwac (to trust with heart) to believe.

ijath when a person is very happy over present not yet received.

ijar, rjar gazelle.

ijec bird something like guinea fowl.

rjec afterwhile; dew; second course of meal.

ijeny ijeny always angry.

qek to cut body to let blood out.

i)er to head dura; secretly; secret; the people had plenty to eat and just wanted to lie around; to soak to become soft; curse, if a thief steals my things and I curse him, he being absent.

qwat qer qer happy, ci locda qer qer m y heart was happy. qet fragment of broken dish; piece of. i) th ashes. jien to sift.

qiu to cut with sharp razor. QIC teacher; knew (past tense of qac). 1)1 n to carry on head. i)ip to sob; sob. qir gossip.

ijir ijir bright and shiny, teke rjir qir. qith brain. rjcar beans. i)0C to call with loud voice; swampy; last of October.)0C, rjec strengthen (imperative). tjok to vomit. ijok- yie ijok- to sigh. ijom, qomni, poss. quom knife. qop to breathe in. ijok rubber tree; Dinka. rj ol first; not late; right away; to spit. tjol, ljuit crippled; lame; (ram ml) cripple; (nei tl ljuit) cripples. ijot, ci wicde rjot crazy. ijote still; yet. rjuarj to pry up; to strike mildly but not let go stick. rjuat not yet finished with food. rjuat ljuat to talk thru nose. rjueny to pick up mud or dirt; cloddy ground; to mix with grass rjueny piny rei kaka; to race ci ne ijueny ke ran we raced with a person. quet fishhook and pole together quet ke guari. ijui poorly as mac pete rjui fire burns poorly.

te war) ke qui qui blinked.

quik hiccough.

quit to scratch.

quk to pass at right angles; to see at a distance; vomitus. quka as kwi quka why. qui cuk heel. qui puk to put ash on. qun-handto. used when something close by is wanted. rwacke e qun qun to whisper. quon to twist and make armlets; to hunt one up rjuone je ciiq emo hunt him in that village. quok to interrupt; to divide; to judge quok rwac; to cut. CA quok piny the conference is finished; to disperse. quot to cut off; to cut; n. boil. CI quot have you passed menopause? quot, qut female. qut to ask about wedding feast; big dance; wedding dance; fish. qut to sharpen bl pencil qut (cutting toward you). qut I these things (when name unknown). qwaaq worn out physically; tired; used as tired of my sins. qwac to smell of; to sniff. qwak, qwak neck, qwak pi.; (sing.) dwor, many things. qwal to borrow; loan; debt. qwale quth bad. qwan four; much. qwandien fourth. qwani (pi.), dwor (sing.) things. qwanke enough; abundant; many. qwat constipation.

teke pau pau ijwath to nurse or care for; (ram mi) nurse. ijwen to provoke eiju ijweni ya mo what do you provoke me (for). ijwcny to escape. ijwet, ijweni suitor; bachelor; young man. I)wet to pull in fishline. I) wet scratch. qwoth to stink; to smell badly; to putrefy. ijyec to teach. qyeceni rode practicing.

-0 as suffix of nown means first to one and then to another.

-0 added to verb means interrogation.

oam to tempt.

oam, oamni n. temptation.

oi to fall off.

om when swollen place, being pressed, is slow to regain shape.

or A to sympathize or A ke par to help in sorrow.

e ou e on tinkling of anklets.

91, Ol hip bone.

ol to pound dura.

oltar altar.

on alright; yes; well!.

ot- to pound dura.

3th to be undecided eiju othl jia mo what are you undecided for.

paal to come to surface. pac newly; new.

pac- to grunt.

pace medium good, used with food only. pai egg white; moon. pai dap woman who has just given birth to child, called this for year or more. paidieth cow which has little calf. pak, cuke pak thin to stay 1 day and 2 nights. pak- to be absent. pak pakni dandruff. paki, pakini merchant. pal to pray. ci palu greeting. pal kwoth church service. pam, pamni stone; rock; mountain. pan volunteer crop of dura; also reoccurrence of yaws. pankeje day before yesterday. pankeje dodien day before day before yesterday. panomka slope but not very high. pap to prepare or spread as table for meal. par to mourn; to sympathize; to lean against. par, pare, parke similar; same as; on an equal. pareni imitating.

parika to jump because frightened. pat to pat; fan used to separate chaff from dura. path banana. patto husk; pau to bleed profusely; profusely; to jump because frightened ce wa pau he jumped because frightened. teke pau pau fear; alarm; to twitch.

payc mut path path pay mut when not yet married a year. pay pay splash. pal to leave alone. pal to ask for counsel; to pierce through. pam leaves fallen to ground; leaves of tree which they eat if very hungry. p At to sharpen. pat grass tray to shake pounded dura in; bran. pat cuka, pat cukni bottom of foot. pat tet, pat tetni metacarpal. pate pat, CI au patc pat earth is full of people. path spirit, usually evil; evil eye; to hasten; to hurry; to stop; to arrest. pec- to seize; to raid. peet collar bone.

pek amount; share; end; number; pek yaa horizon. limit.

pek rwitka term of pregnancy. pek runika life. mi th 11 pek everlasting; eternal. pel cunning; n. cunning; deceitful; clever. pel pel, pel pell rabbit; sandfly. ram mi pel pel, brilliant person: deceiver; nei tl pel pel (pi.). pen to fall.

penh to forbid; to withhold. pet, peet small, black fish. pet- to burn; n. January (when grass is burned). pi, poss. pin I water, always used in plural form only. pic to twirl; to spin; (bi mac) to start fire.

pick when grass is moved by fish so you know they are there and can spear them. pick- to stable. pien wasp; poisonous green snake (black spotted). pier, pier sty or ulcer in eye. pier, pien fish trap, pik to adorn; funnel. pil rolling pin; stone used to grind dura on; d3 pil small stone used as grinder. pim to hit with hand; to hit with spear and cannot release spear. pith to grow up; growth. pith, pilthni maternity belt. piu sweet milk; fresh. piwit, piwi(t)ni slingshot. piar, plan scar. pi I) to listen intently; to be silent; no grass; bare ground, piny down; ground. CI piny kap no wind; calm, pith to splice. poan, poss. pun rice stalk; headpad made of ricestalks. poc to wipe; to sweep with hand, ce pok e pok entirely finished with food. pon to gather lots of fruit, po lit rain during dry season. pal to be ashamed ci ran pol a person was ashamed. pol

pol winner. pot to leave because afraid; to break; to blow. poteka to put on. poth smooth; (e te) very smooth; to bless. poth poth level; smooth.

poth poth ram mi bee iwac poth poth to be entirely finished with food. pual rested; to give food to newly married woman. puat side meat; fat of meat. puath small cow. puath, puoth, poss. puothni lung. puc to be ashamed; shame; cike puoc they are not ashamed. puk to pour into another pan. pup, pul, poss. pwol pool. pul potato; small hole in ground in which head rests while tribal marks are cut. pulke to float. pum wai) cheek bone and forehead also. pun, certain kind of fish. pun I bead girdle worn by men. puom to pick one here and one there. puon to gather cotton; to pick out seeds. puok to be finished. puol unlucky.

ram mi puol puol fast runner. puote excelling; surpassing. puot made him afraid; to play instrument; to beat drum. puot to jump away; to slip away; to fear. puot puot small animal. puot rar to cast off. puotc angry, puoteni nei toto we are angry at those people. puoth gift, used with food only; to bless; n. blessing. puoth thok tongue-tied; cannot enunciate clearly. pur skull; hoe; mark or track; to cultivate.

pur JAr, pur JAri shoulder blade. puth to cover; to smell badly; to give many descendants; small piece of animal skin, puth to pull apart; to pick; flesh on lower part of thigh. puth puth bad; very dirty; foul smelling. puth to fasten.

puk, poss. puka cow manure ashes. puluka row boat. pun, punni, poss. puna or punka triangular piece of sheepskin as woman's loincloth, worn in front. pwar to swell up; to boil; to rise; to ferment; cloud; sky. pwar, pwor waterbuck. pwony, pwany body. pwony- to praise with song. pwok to bathe. pwol swamp. pwolc to be healthy; to steal food; to be light of weight; to be strong. mi pwol pwol- light of weight. pwolka sound (adj.). pwol pwony jok exceedingly safe and sound. pwot, to swell; put is one form. pwoth to husk; to shuck. pwoth tet clean hands.

ral noise.

ram, ran, pi. rem person.

rami person who.

ram mi bac slovenly person.

ram mi bee Iwac thief.

ret- ram mi cok stingy person.

ram mi cum cum lovable person.

ram midit, nei tidit adult.

ram mi ket, nei ti ket, ji keta swimmer.

ram mi kwil, nei ti kwil thief.

ram mi kwiny bully.

ram mi ce dwor lokelorj abhorrer.

ram mi luake, ji lueke helpmeet; helper; partner.

ram mi mith mith one who eats lots.

ram mi muc cheerful giver.

ram mi Ia nup, nei ti Ia nup messenger.

ram mi pel pel clever person; artist; cheat.

ram mi raij one who shoots well.

ram mi riarj rial) rich person.

ram mi nij ni) one who hurries.

ram mi rio very fat man.
ram mi roth one who seemingly does underhand work; bully.
ram mi thek worshipper.
ram mi ca yen, nei ti ca yen prisoner.
ram mi yuoi drunkard.
ran buth guide.
ran gorka, ji gorka pupil; student.
ran JAl, jl jal visitor; traveler.
ran lat, jl lat worker; employee.
ran moija, jl moija, jl moijka visitor; guest.
ranh close by; yet to come; still outside; wants to come bl yan ranh dwil (I want to come in the house).
ran, temporal region.
rai) flash of lightning; light.
wa rarj to make a shadow.
raij one who shoots well.
rar abroad; away; outside; limitless.
rathe very small fish that little boys catch.
rau thirst.
rak, rake nyal when two men want same girl.
ral tendon; vein; ligament; artery.
ral cwoth guinea worm.
ral dual) tendon of Achilles.
ral wuom bridge of nose.
ram long-legged insect.
ral) scar where skin has not gotten black again.
rap rap membrane; tallow; covering of lung.
rath to hasten; to come and go repeatedly.
rec, rec, poss. rac, fish.
rec pacifier; to pacify; to make peace.
rec cua when first child a boy.
rec nyal when first child a girl.
reco inside.
reu two.
reet to tear.
rek poss. reek enclosure.
rek- rwac to interrupt conversation.
rel white ants that like wood and grass, too.
rel hillock; different; no resemblance.
remde his soldiers.
rep to add to; to give repeatedly; to increase; n. increase; worm.
rep rep sheer; thin; soft (material).
ret to pass through; to go ahead.
ret, retni, poss. reet orphan.
ret, reet razor blade.

ret- part to go one path, part another, meeting later.

ret ke tok to laugh heartily.

rial) abundance; plenty; rich; enough; to abound. riaij rial) shiny; rich, riar to perish; fool: unclean: senseless. riar cai) almost sunset. riat torch, riau to scatter as to go to different homes: to dazzle: to light up. rial. riall half dollar; two shillings. rial- to let come to ground slowly to clear away; to prepare. rial bek, rial bekni bird with red bill, larger than maribou. ric age or class: peacemaker: to dodge. rie to twist; to roll: to return. riec to be curly (ca ro riec) it twisted itself. rieke, riaka he is busy; I am busy. mi riel color. rielni undone. riem blood; child one month old or less. riem gwac- abortion; to abort. rieny meningitis. riep to hurry. riet to be silent (ce bl riet) he will not rule (or talk). riet, rietnl law; order; rule. rio coarse part of dura; bran, rit to turn.

loc rit to repent, ci loc rit he repented. be rill to leave regular path and go by sidepath. riu name of tree; to turn part away; to hurt inside; to blink as blinded by sun; breadth; (yaa) north; (yaa) south.

riak crested crane.

riak altar.

riak work; business; false trust; concern; to be concerned about; to work; to be busy. rial) k A sandy place. rik, nkni n. row. ril to run or pierce into flesh. riny to straighten out; to extend. ril) meat; to hurry. ril) duol) meat without bones. riijl n. running. rini nhial flight. rip very tall; very big; to refuse to do assigned work. rip certain insect; bug. rip, riup finger or toe nails; claws. rir poisonous snake, red and brown; restless; to fly away (used with birds only). nth to make a shadow. ro, ruth hippopotamus. ro ro certain kind of ant. roan bath famine. roc to swallow; to devour; fishspear with hook to catch fish. rok cell; segment. rok cow with spreading horns, tips almost meeting. rol, rul, poss. rol country. rol throat; alimentary tract; pimples. rol childless woman; sterile woman, will not adopt child unless relative. Rol Bunyni Abbysinia. Rol Ker Dinka Land. Rol Rip Egypt. rol rol in haphazard way; when food is not cooked well teke rol rol. rom to hold; to care for; to guard.

rwil rom gat guardian.

rom locdu cheer up.

rop to string beads.

ro, ro self.

roath, roth ear of corn.

rok, ruk kidney.

rok to entangle.

rok, poss. ruok grass rope.

rok, rokni grasshopper.

rol withered; dried up.

rorj, rorj seed; pit.

rorj to squeeze in; to fit in.

ror big lizard.

ror child not yet weaned.

roth whirlwind; cyclone; axilla.

roth to plaster with mud.

ram mi roth, nei-ti roth idiot.

rol when tribal mark scars will be big someday bike rol. rual flock; herd. ruam, rum seroot fly. mam, poss. ruamni big sheep. man opening at back of nose. ruany, rony cane stalk. mat to snore. mau- to jump high in dancing; to serenade. rual syphilis.

rub A quarter dollar; shilling. ruec, cikc ro ruec they crowded against themselves; to crowd against; (wic-) to forget. ruck to put on. met to shine in ci car) waijda ruct the sun shone in my eye. ruct to take armlets and anklets off. ruit to drink milk. ruk to tie grass across path so one will trip over it; to splice but connecting place shows.

ruk, ruk double tooth.

rum to meet (always takes pi.

subject); to splice. rumcidwar, rumcidwan porcupine. rum ka(k)ni boundary line, rum puth, rum puthni ibis; sacred ibis. rui to give to all; to distribute to all. ruony to point out with tongue; to feel way in dark; to protrude thru opening. ruot when cow wont let milk down. ruok to pay fine for illegitimate child, (4 cows are paid and then father may claim child). ruok ruok noise of boiling. ruon. rui). piny c ruoi) run. earth is round, ruoth to fight; to bite and throw its body; to spear; (ruth is one form). rup, rwop, poss. rwop forest. rup rup working or walking hard or fast. rur mirage. rut to cry; n. cry. rut brave.

rut jec gas rumbling in bowels. rwac word; to speak; speech; to talk; talk. rwac kwen betrothal. rwac parka parable. rwath young ox. rwath thak mi puath small steer. rwei spittle; saliva. rwei kak phlegm. rweth to drink milk. rwil Nile perch, white fish, delicious. rwil spring; planting season; first part.

rwit tiel rwit to be pregnant.

rwith certain kind of fish.

rwitka pregnancy.

rwon run year.

rwot boy's name.

ryei, ryath poss. ryai, ryathni boat.

ryei nath dugout canoe.

ryei nhial aeroplane.

tac, tec ant.

teke tai wrinkled.

tai wee wrinkles.

tak spleen.

tak to braid; pain and swelling in breast. tak A tike, teke I have, you have, he has. tame pany immediately. tanye- to rub dry. tar), turj long stick. tap tobacco; unfertile ground. tap tl nuor nuor fine tobacco which they pound. tar bottom; under; (wi(c)dli) hold head back; foundation. tar bap white bead worn by men. taripe tariffe. tat, tatnl hipbones. tayou- big lake. tak Saviour. tak muol, tak muall kneecap; patella. tal, tel calf of leg. tat on purpose kan yith ke tat (I did not spear on purpose. tat Shullik.

tath to mold; to form; big spear; mold; form. te are; is; to abide; to stay. ten to be finished ci retni dial wa ten the razor blades are all finished. ten I nhial very far away in sky. teno many days ahead. teny to ache, used with earache. teny sun shining after rain. tea to hide; to deceive. teeth to be happy; (Iwac) happiness. tek, tekni silver or lead bracelets. tek tek to have none left at all. tel when grass moves showing there is something in it; to wag. tern to bring part of them; to kill fish; to cut; to separate (wa tern); to fish at river early a. m.; n. cut. tenh to start out on return trip. tel) papyrus; crack of lightning; to pound to get dust out: to dust: to shake: to free himself: to scramble away. tel to execute this rite which is called thiai). ter, jl teer enemy. ter to distend as balloon blown up tet to dig. as ce ter.

tet, tetni hand. tetar certain kind of fish. teth to start; to fall. tier to fish with fishing spear only; to stomp in water so fish will think there are other fish there and come. tiel white-eared cob; miserly. tiel jealous; jealousy used with women only; cyek mi teke tiel, wife who has jealousy.

WA tiel mitot

WA tiel to have plenty; enough; ce WA tiel he had plenty. tiel) earthquake. tiep wooden shield (not ambatch) carried in dance. tier to remember ci wicda tier, tiet, poss. tietka understanding: wisdom: sorcerer; (lat) sorcery. tieth to pour a little on. tieth e cuet very hot; red hot. tik cloudy. tik, poss. tika- chin. tlk tik or tek tek ticking of clock. tik, tiak beads.

til A clear; to see thru clear water. tim to revere: to be homesick for: to honor. tim to remember. tiol twaar sugar. tiak yolk of egg. tial, til earring. tiam to be famished; to starve; starvation. tiap, poss. tipka shade; shadow. tiar to come and find it already in progress (used with dance only). tiat pulp or fiber. tiath to break (as dishes). tiath- to itch. tie spirit (of heart); crystalline lens; (waij) pupil of eye; sight. tiec to pull; buildings; (jok) to shrink; close to ground; to draw up closer. tlek finely pounded dura. tlep tlep fertile as fertile ground. tlk, poss. teeka life. t iked I a me chin whiskers. til, til person who knows Nuer well.

CI nhial dam e tim tim tosprinkle rain. tin pi. of in- the. tl nor) piny somersault. tin win those of the past; long ago. tl nyin go very fine; very good. tl nyin ijwan many; abundance. tl nyin tieni many little. tltl these. tlth raw. tok, poss. toka jabiru; bird that stays rar in desert or uninhabited place. CI to I ll greeting (secondary). torn- to put mouth to water to drink. torn torn broad bladed grass growing along river; noise of fish as rec teke torn torn, tony, poss. tuny pipe. tor white ants that eat wood only; swamp. toe certain kind of white dura; to lie down. mi toe green; (yil) green and yellow; (mi yil toe) blue. tol) manure pile used as smudge in barn; to be born dead; to die; to pierce grass into ear as CA jlthda tor) I pierced my ear. toij, till) wood to burn; sticks; handle of spear; fuel. tor) manytapni, tun, manytapni corns-toi) ewer mushroom. talk.

tor) rul trachea. toroi), toror) tonsil. tot planting season; from May to September; croak of frog. mitot, titot; tl torn; tl nyin tieni small; little.

toto twith, twithni toto, those; tlti those at a distance. tuac to put to bed as to put child to bed; to not butt in; value. tual to blister; n. blister. tuAl, tuah lotus (or is it thual (V)). tuany certain kind of fish. tuat grass used to make rope. tuc to pop out; to spring out; el pi tuc spring of water (literally water sprang out). tuk to order out; to discharge (one form is tuok); to finish. tuk tuk to pop; to have popping sound as teke tuk tuk. tuk tukni popcorn. tul to break (used with wood); does not mean to shatter. tul to pick dura by the handsful or to gather dura heads by hand. tul- to make; to cut wood certain size; to gather as tuli many-tap ni; you gather corn. turn to butt into. turn turn Adam's apple; trachea. tuny to smoke out ca nyith tuny ke mac I smoked mosquitoes out with fire. tun. perfect place (thlie mi jyek thin); false fear; cob; vacant as no one here. tut), tuoi horn of animal. tuij baijto false fear. tuij club. tuoc to count. tuom to disperse; to turn back to back; to pierce but not thru entirely. tuok to start. tuol smoke; CA tuol I hunted and hunted.

tuoij part.

tup to be very rich; sufficient; to have plenty. tur sandstorm; dust; to scare up lots of animals. turuk, turukni light colored foreignor. tut, poss. twot male; ox. tut deel ram. tut gar name of Nuer omnipresent god. tuth to protect blade of spear; to join together as bike yua WA tuth will join grass skirt together. tutluet brother of the fox. tut man palck, tut man palckni rooster; cock. twaar bees. twac, twacni, poss. twacka skin of animal; loincloth of skin. twac kwac leopard skin. twai twai spinal cord. twak mud. twai) wee top of head where hair circles. twany to make pressure, twar dates; honey; syrup; to chant; to sing dance song. twat, twani wild goose. twer to scrape burnt or dried food out of kettle; to curette (one form is twir). ce twer e twer entirely finished with food. twiny to pinch.

twil to blister; to break promise, twith A sorcery; the work of medicine man as lat twith A. twith, twithni drumstick.

twoc thindik twoc, poss. twicka box made of mud. twom, turn, poss. tumka hypodermic or intravenous injection. twoi), tui) egg. twok, kwaka dish. twok- to sing child to sleep; to praise; to comfort child. twol to reoccur as ce le nyok it reoccurred or el botde twol the sore reoccurred. twot fontenal. twoth to polish.

tha clock; watch.

thac mist; vine; moisture; dew; headpad; Nuer pillow for women; also pillow for newly gar-ed boys.

thactt, thacitni sudani washtub.

thadup hand dipping irrigation system.

thagia waterwheel for irrigation.

thailo Shiloh.

thai nyany to be magnified.

thak ox; cooking pot; v. to carry in hand.

thaklai) metal dish; finger bowl.

thai to heat; to cook.

thalcal) middle of morning.

than part of; some.

tharjwarj crosseyed.

mi thar last year.

ml thar ke je year before last.

mi thar ke rwil last spring.

tharal, tharali camel.

thar bap big, white bead.

thar lee root of tooth.

that- to put food on fire; to cook.

Thamuel Samuel.

than certain kind of fish.

thap below level of surface.

thee to splash; to dip out; much afraid; to tremble ce dwal A CI jecde WA thee
he feared so his abdomen trembled. thek to worship; holiness; hallowed; holy; v. to
menstruate. them basket to measure dura in. ther to whittle; to sharpen; to bless; man
whose wife is pregnant; enmity; pregnant woman. thi- to strain: to filter. thiam, thim
sneeze; v. thiam- to sneeze. thiarj afternoon; v. to fill; antelope; name of rite used
to appease god when woman is impregnated when child is still nursing; full. thiap
to examine; to touch. thiau ke mer to cry tears; te war) ke thiau thiau tearful. thiec,
thieeni question. thiec- to ask.

thiet grass used to make grass skirt. thiel temple of head. thier grass used to make
doors. thik, thiakni door. thim to cut off pieces; ca rirj thim I cut meat in pieces. thio
thio always winking eyelids; sparkling. thiol fat of meat. thiarj ciirj nath hartebeast.
thill I k wire; wireless station. thin, thin female breast. thin there is, (contraction of at
hi n). thindik corncob.

thip thyake eliq thip to limp; to change one's mind; to distribute; to relinguish; to
divide among; to give one's life for another. thir, thier pillar of house; rafters. thok,
thuk valve; message; letter; mouth. thok, thuk language. thok jak, thok jakni blanket.
thok JUOC harelip. thok kal gate; gateway. thok kwe old but still good. thok Iwac pit
of stomach. thok nhial; thok piny upper lip; lower lip. thok thin, thuk thinni nipple.
thok war) swamp. thok wan mouth or bank of river, thol snake. thoi), poss. thurjka
place where dura is pounded. thoij to murder; to heap up. thol to collect; to summon;
sound of hard wind in spring. thor to mix; to sharpen; to dilute milk. thou same as
wild dates. thol warm.

thol to bend and bend. thol- to sit in sunshine outside; to be fooled. thol- to put it
on as tholl mith wic tebal, put food on table. ce ro thol as old person, whose strength
is gone. thoij, thon. wildcat. thor brittle; crumbly; swampy pasture. thot to be silent.
thot to pass gas.

-thu-in-law; balie thu unseasoned; tasteless. thuac large earthern vessel to store
dura in. thuak finished (used with food), thuany certain deep sea animal. thuai)
dimples. thuc to hoe part of field and leave part not hoed. thuc manytapni ear of corn,
thuk to destroy; to be fulfilled; to be finished. thuke thin.

thu I klir bends of river. thun jor to never reach, thuny to push. thuij to jump out
and away; murder; already; dead; to receive fines for murder cases. thuokklen their
beginning. thuom small crowd; organ; musical instrument. thuol to search; to spy.
thuop poss. thuopa yeast; bricks. thural, thurall pants; trousers. thure to sound in
order to find hidden door; to destroy. thut- one class of Nuers, possibly 75 80 years
old now. thut to tow; to tug; to stretch; to pull harpoon back. thut, thutni nail. thut
kul certain constellation of stars. thuk, thuk Iwac, thuk indit aorta. thwaar to float:
dates: honey. thwom sterile woman. thwok truth. thyake close by: easy. thyake el
in. brimful.

thyckc"

thyekc heavy.

thyeke eliqo very strong.

uy in order that; since; because.

uorje open.

uth big basket like bushel basket.

wa exclamation.

waale this year.

waao to burn.

waat, waatni whip (like blacknake whip). wac wet; to be wet. pi ti wac wac acid. wacc tart; sour. wac rac part of fish. wai-, wath relative. waide bottom. wain wine. wak to pluck: to ache: to call loudly; clatter: to balk: to throb: to cry out. wal or daf) wal ten. wal wicde kel eleven. wal wicde reu twelve. wal wicde dyok thirteen. wal wicde ijwan fourteen. wal wicde dhyec fifteen. wal wicde bakel sixteen. wal wicde baro seventeen. wal wicde badak eighteen. wal wicde baijwan nineteen. walllen tenth. wal wicde kellien eleventh. wal, wall puddles.

4 Huffman, Nuer-English wal medicine; charm; amulet. wal dhicu opiate; sedative. wal ml kop kop incense; perfume. wal nuirka medicine as charm to restore life. wal mi qwanyke perfume; incense. wal dwar or wal doar laxative. wale today.

ni wale in a very short time. wan to surround: to steal: to be very dirty: to wither so they die; fox; thief; new grass that has just come up. wany when sky is cloudy; clouds scattered. wany to move; to replace; to exchange; rope or belt around waist; armlet. wany piny to roll over on ground. waij, nym eye. waij wrath: swamp: grain; waij I wac anger. waij kwura, wan, kwun wrist. waij cwa, waij cwani joints of body. warjda idiom meaning my body. waij pumka riverbank; waij pumka kwicimi opposite river bank. wai) cuopka ankle bone. cue lar I ml waij to affirm emphatically. loc wai) to be wrathy ci locda wai) my heart was wrathy. cwa wai) cheekbone. war night; wardar, ci war dit (the night is big) midnight. war lip about supper time ci war lip the night waited. wan shoes.

war war little morsels. wat to take dirt out of hole.

tc wat wat illegible like chicken scratches'. wat to push into; to take out; to search thru. watak certain kind of white dura. wath horsefly; one who always wants to fight; inlet in river; landing place for boats; tall grass; watering place at river; gnat; riverbank. wath pus came out. as oe wath pus came out. wau wauni glossy ibis. waudc grass in cow's stomach. WA went; ban WA we two will go; bane WAI and all of you will go; n. going. WAdin title of respect used by older person toward younger man: same as gatda (my son). WAl fruit: garden products: to be nauseated. WAl to be disturbed (el pi ro WAl) (water moved itself); to be moved; to chew cud. WAn you and I go; wane (pi.), you (pi.) and I go. WAr certain vegetable; grass that is eaten. WAr manure. WAr- to search. wea girls to be dancing before men

Clkc we A they danced before the men. wee village with cattle but no fields: town: city. wc to answer: to say: to exclaim: to get: to call out. Wea go, 2nd. pers. pi. imper. of wir.

wcl to be finished CA ro wel it was finished.

wer to sow: to scatter.

wernyin, wernyinni window.

Wet to beckon.

weth disease, somewhat like syphilis but of different origin.

wet wet to go to fight ce te wet wet he went to fight.

wi to warn; to call all the people.

wic on; above.

wic, wieni, poss. wee village.

wic, wath, poss. wee, wathni head.

wi(c)-ruec to forget.

wi(c) car to think.

wic dwil, wath dwilli roof.

wic JAra clavicle.

wic mwon grave.

wic wuka, wath wani shoulder.

wie to cry; n. warning.

will Nuer god.

WIl to play; to deny; to be distrustful; to circle around; to encircle; to go around; to make repeated trips; to fear each other wile ro.

wile nath to fool people as sound of boat.

win to go around (not on regular path).

winith where.

wir, wea, wa to go.

Win long horned (cattle) yok tl Win.

Wit to sharpen.

With, wi(th)eni club with big head.

wituorj on edge of crowd.

woe to put out; to empty out.

WOC dhol to make the tribal marks.

ci riem woe to abort.

wor chase; race; to chase; to race; sore on heel, possibly bruised originally, gwath ml ca yieth, cc k bee place which I pierced, it hurt again, ou noise of boat coming; chug chug; echo. wok baldheaded; to fade as ci bid c wok the color is faded. wok, wok upper arm. wop to sprain. WOt generosity. WOth misfortune will come; to be spilt; blood flowed to ground, ci riem woth. wuc to break out in heat, wul to lean against; to open path. wum, wuum, poss. wuom nose. wum juoc cleft palate. wum kcluqka neck of squash; class name given boys whose tribal marks were cut in 1925 (also called cai yatni). wum kiir head of gourd, wun to distend. wuony to disagree; to argue; to wrangle. wuok to loosen by working it back and forth. wuoth to locate open place for entrance; to tiptoe; to quake. wut, wum poss. wutka man. wut poss. wot ostrich. wut generous. wut mi bee miser. wut kur warrior.

wuth to cut; to make small opening. wun dark clouds; cloudy.

yai exclamation of disgust.

yak to discard; to throw away; to upset; to run the washing machine. yak, yaak hyena. yak- to sift; to shake dura to get fine out. yaktoi certain very thin fish. yal to tangle up; to jumble up. yal to exclaim; to refuse cc yal, he refused. yal, to be crosseyed; ci waijke yal, his eyes crossed. yal yal to roll the eyes as tekc yal yal. ro Ic yal to go to bad place. yal dwil eaves of house. yam to walk where there is no road; failing sight. yaij, yok, poss. yande, cow. yai) mi mar dark red cow. yar mad; to refuse: worn out: sterile (used with people only). yar- leckc teke yar- spaces between. yat- to soil as rat soils clothes. yat rough as yat jok rough back; butter; married womans dress made of sheepskin a two piece suit (see yet), yath yath region between hipbones and ribs. yath stroke; grass used for tying; tender grass; to keep hitting or pricking repeatedly. yath high jumping fish. yath to snatch away, yuth is one form; to kneel as ce mal- yath piny, he knelt on ground. 01 ro yal to want exact information. yam yatn scratchy. yat, yet finger; toe. yec yec expression of surprise or praise.

yeny yuanke yeny to extinguish.

yeny to dry dishes; to wipe.

yek, poss. yika grass mat.

yd to chase.

yem to strike at; cu ken e yem they hit it. yen to bandage; to dress a wound; to tie: to imprison. yene you and, as jin yene Dei), you and Del), yet married woman's dress, yet-triangular piece of sheep skin worn in back, pun- triangular piece of sheepskin worn in front. yeth ciiq newly made village. yeth to go on; to be unacquainted with path; to move; to remove; to arrive, yeth A rough. yic to be dumbfounded; to be bewildered; to be dizzy, yien to stop; to herd; shepherd. yik Nuer altar. yio certain kind of red dura; fish with three horns. yiu asthma. yi, ye you (pi.). yiath to sacrifice. yie spirit; (e bee) to breath heavily: to sigh yie ijok; breath; air. yiec, yieeni to sweep: broom. yier, yien garner. yier- to grease. yik to destroy; to be empty handed; to go aimlessly. yik pual to be ashamed to eat in front of sweetheart. yik yik rattle for child; te yik yik has rattling (sound). mi yil light green; blue.

yil yil twirling.

yil to spear at fish and miss; leaf of lotus, may be eaten: yil nhial lightning. yilblth certain class of Nuers of long ago, all dead now. mi yil wal purple. yir, yiri, poss. yier river, yir to anoint; much pain or suffering. yit game played with mud balls. waij yitka, yit mud balls to play game with. yit- to throb or to sting. yith pneumonia.

yith, yo, poss. yoni money; metal. yitklen head of dura minus grains. yo spear and fishing spear; weapons. yo dwop toll tax. yoc to drag. yor- to throw. yoij cry of crow; madman; to be drunk. yoi) yoij mad; crazy; cike nij yoi) yoi) they ran like mad or crazy. yot to shoot; to strike; to throw at; to hit; to pull trigger. yot- to make dry skin (on body) come off. yot yot membrane. yot yot, yot yotni page of book. yoth to yearn for; to be eager for. yua short grass skirt. yuac to drag out; to tow; to caress and praise; to pull out. yuai to feel with hand. yuak to move as leaves move in wind, teke yuak. yual to yell; to exclaim. yuanke branches of tree.

ywak yuc to go to gather wood.

yum, yumni, poss. yumka dish made of gourd, yum matha cup. yum ryei nhial aluminum. yuop to favor.

yuop- ro to guard self from evil. yuot topknot of bird, yuot to kill.

yuothcikcrwacdcyuoth to interrupt; cike rwacde yuoth they interrupted his words.

yure to take hold.

yut, yutni certain small, short bird.

yuth to pull; to anticipate words; to gasp.

yup- to puff; to pant.

ywak beard.

Notes on Grammar.

Nouns. Formation of plural. By adding suffix-m to singular form.

miak miakni insect nen nenni mirror nyeu nyeuni cat nyik nyikni the fellow wife

Nouns ending in k may form the plural by adding the suffix-ni (The suffix I seems to be used only with nouns ending in r or I as far as I have found examples.) By change in intonation.

By substituting u for wo.

kwoth kuth god kwor kur hundred dwop dup path twom turn hypodermic injection dwoi) dun. shell of ostrich egg.

Nouns whose singular form ends in t, may drop the final t before adding the suffix-ni to form the plural.

mut muni spear gumut gumuni owl kwut kwuni suitor ijwct ijweni bachelor dit dim roofer

Some nouns form their plurals irregularly.

yai) y 3 cow twok kwaka dish yith yo money or metal wai) nin eye cyck man wife Gender.

Gender is often indicated by stating whether the thing mentioned is male or female.

tut male ljuot female wuni men man women dhol boy nyal girl

The word tut may be placed before the word to indicate gender as tut dccl male sheep, or they may say del athin, e jcn quot meaning there is a sheep, it is a female.

The prefixes nya- and nyan- always indicate feminine gender.

River banks, the earth and the sky are all considered masculine if one it to judge from the riddles they ask as mar tut tidit dai) reu (guess two big males) is answered by riverbanks or the earth and sky.

The moon is often called nyapai which would indicate feminine gender.

Case.

Nouns ending in k, add the suffix-A for the singular form and-ni for the plural when used as object of a preposition.

The suffix-ill, added to the singular form of the noun, is used to form all cases in the plural.

kak kaka ka(k)ni field guk guka gu(k)ni pocket cuk cuka cukni foot kok koka ko(k)ni grave

Nouns whose vowel is form these cases as object of a preposition by lengthening the.

del deel sheep (singular) det deet sheep (plural) ret reet razor blade eel ceel certain fish

Some nouns whose vowel is u, form these cases in the singular number by substituting wo for u, the plural cases being formed by adding the suffix-ni to the singular form of the noun.

rup rwop rupni forest mun mwon ground tut twot tutnl male

Many nouns may be governed by these rules but there are many, the rules governing which, I have not yet found.

Pronouns.

Declension of Personal Pronouns

First person

Nominative y n I kon we

Possessive-da,-Ia,-ka my-dan,-Un,-kon our Objective y A me 0 us -ka and-kon in the possessive indicate a plural noun.

Second person

Nominative jin you yen

Possessive-du,-lu,-ku your-dun,-lun,-kun Objective jl you ye -ku and-kun in the possessive case indicate a plural noun.

Third person

Nom. jen he, she, it ken they

Poss.-de,-le,-ke his, hers, its-dien,-lien,-klen their Obj. je him, her, it ke them -ke and-klen in the possessive case indicate a plural noun.

The possessive forms-Ia,-lu and-le in the singular and-Un,-lun and-lien in the plural are used when the final consonant of the noun they follow is I.

-da and-I a indicate that both the possessor and the possessed are singular.-ka indicates that the possessor is singular and the possessed plural.-dan and-IAn indicate that the possessors are plural and the possessed singular.

-kon indicates that both possessors and possessed are plural. No gender is recognized in the pronouns, the same form being used for all. The personal pronoun may be used as a suffix to the root form of a verb as Singular

First person-A gura I want

Second person-I gun you want

Third person- gure he wants

Plural

First person-kon,-ko gurkon, gurko we want Secons person-e gure you want

Third person-ke gurke they want In these cases, no other subject need be expressed unless desired.

Relative pronouns.

mi often introduces a relative clause. If ml is the subject of the relative clause, it is followed by CI or bl.

c jcn thokde citke rip mi bi nyith kc yok rei gwop leini, (it is its mouth resembling a needle which the mosquito pushes in the animal's skin.) ml is often used with a time clause of future condition.

mi jin bi yai) jik, noni je.

(If you find a cow, bring her.) mi condition meaning "if".

mi dwul lapm dial citeke dwil erne, kwoan dial bike liu, (If all rice houses resembled this house, all the rats would die.) me introduces time clause of completed action.

me ci lony ben, Debid ce iju lei?

(When the lion came, what did David do?)

Adjectives.

The comparative form of adjectives is formed by adding the suffix-ni to the positive form. The superlative is formed by using the phrase "surpassing them in (quality mentioned)".

Positive

Comparative

Superlative

Positive

Comparative

Superlative good better surpassing them in goodness bigger he is bigger than all of them.

gwaa gwaam lenye kc ke goie dit ditm ditni jen ke kcndial Adjectives usually follow the nouns they modify as dwil inbor e dwil midit. House the white is house a big. The white house is a big house. in- (singular) and tin (plural) are prefixes used to designate some particular quality as yai) inbor the white cow yok tinbor the white cattle. in and tin usually follow the noun and preceed the adjective they they designate.

ml (singular) and tl (plural) are prefixes used when nothing definite is designated as yai) mibor a white cow yok tlbor white cattle They occupy the same position in the sentence as in and tin.

Verbs.

Regular form of conjugation. gur- to want

Present tente I want gurkon, gurneini 1st. person gur- a 2nd. 3d.

person gur-person gur- you want gur- e he, she, it, wants gur- kc we want, wanting you want they want

The 1st. person plural gur nei ni is often contracted to gureni.

1st. person CA gur I wanted 2nd. person ci gur 3d. person cc gur

Past tense cako gur cike gur we wanted

Future tense 1st. person ba gur I will want bako gur 2nd. person bl gur be gur 3d. person be gur bike gur we will want

The object of the verb is usually placed between the two words which form the verb as ca je gur mccpan ba je gur irun cal to call luak- to help lak- to wash I wanted him yesterday. I will want him tomorrow.

qac to know ger to row gor to write and many other verbs are conjugated in this same way.

Conjugation of irregular verbs.

bir come Present tense I come, I am coming you come, you are coming he, she, it, is coming we are coming you come, you are coming they come jen is often used in the 3d. person singular when person is nearby. Literally, it means "he is".

we came

Plural 1st. person bako ben, bl nei ben we will come 2nd. person bl yen ben 3d. person bike ben Imperative 2nd. person singular bir 2nd. person plural bca (used when people are nearby). 2nd. person plural bia (used when people are at a little distance).

Conjugation of e to be

Present tense Singular 1st. person e yan or y An e I am 2nd. person e jin or jin e you are 3d. person e jen or jen e he, she, it, is

Plural 1st. person kon e we are 2nd. person yen e you are 3d. person ken e they are

Past tense Singular 1st. person y An e WAneme meedan I was here awhile ago 2nd. person jin e WAneme meedan you were here awhile ago 3d. person jen e WAneme meedan he, she, it, was here awhile ago

Plural 1st. person kon e WAneme meedan we were here awhile ago 2nd. person yen e WAneme meedan you were here awhile ago. 3d. person ken e WAneme meedan they were here awhile ago Some word expressing past time is used as meedan in this case.

Some word expressing future time is usually used as Bi kon e waneme irun we will be here tomorrow.

Verbs Formation of Negative forms.

The negative form often to European ears resembles the regular form of verb, the only difference being in intonation.

Clke WA X they went cf ke wa they did not go

CA wa I went CA V wa I did not go ca gur v I wanted ca x gur v I did not want.

In other cases, kan and ken (not) and their various forms are used.

Negative Form of Conjugation.

Present or future tense. Singular 1st. person CA bi ben I am not coming, or I will not come.

2nd. person CI bl ben you are not coming, or you will not come.

3d. person ce bl ben he, she, it, is not coming, or will not come Plural 1st. person kon cane bl ben, kanko ben we will not come, or have not come 2nd. person yen CA bl ben you will not come 3d. person ken cike bl ben they will not come

Past tense

Singular 1st. person yan kan ben I did not come 2nd. person jin ken I ben you did not come 3d. person jen kene ben he, she, it, did not come

Plural 1st. person kon kanko ben we did not come 2nd. person yen kene ben you did not come 3d. person ken kenke ben they did not come

Prepositions.

The possessive form of the noun is used to indicate when the noun is the object of the preposition "of" as wic wot head of ostrich

This same form of noun is used when the noun is the object of anv preposition but in most cases the preposition is expressed.

Formation of Sentences.

The object of the verb often preceeds the verb.

Ci wan rwacdien hn.

The fox heard their words.

wan is the subject.

CI III) is the vexb.

rwacdien is the object. As in the above sentence, when CI introduces a sentence, the first noun following is the subject, the second noun is the object and both preceed the verb.

In sentences where ce is part of the verb form, the subject is always expressed first, being separated from the object by ce, the verb being last.

wan ce rwacdien III). The adjective usually follows the noun it modifies as

Nyai) ce yarj inbor cam crocodile cow the white ate.

crocodile ate the white cow. The verb may be omitted as mecdan thlle ticl meaning "long ago no jealousy."

ku and kule are used in narrative for rhythm only and always preceed the verb.

Cu wan ku wa rei yika.

fox went in grass mat.

Ce y a kulc, juk wir nhiam".

He me said, "go ahead". mo is used for emphasis.

C jen thwok mi ba lara ji mo.

Is it truth which I will tell you.

It is truth which I will tell you.-0 as suffix to a verb means interrogation.

Jin ci rwacdien hqo?

You their words heard?

Did you hear their words.-0 as suffix to noun means first to one and then to another.

Ce wa ka ramo, cc wa ka ramo.

He went to a person, he went to a person.

He went to one person and then another. In a series of names, use ke for "and" except for the final "and", use mani.

Pec ke Dhiel ke Nyaq kc Dak mani Gaac.

Pec and Dhiel and Nyaq and Dak and Gaac.

(In this instance, the ke takes the place of a comma.) Sentences are short, new sentences being used instead of using many connectives.

Ci kun le ben. Cue thik thiap.

The rat came again. It examined the door.

Cue jik a bum etet. Cue pal.

It found it very hard (or tight). It left. A fact is often stated negatively, modifying it by the next sentence.

Ci gatda liu.

My child died.

Ci dwothni yie mi durj tit.

Is left spirit a very little or a very little life is left.

1784971V000048/43/P

LaVergne, TN USA
07 April 2010